THE MERRY WIVES OF WINDSOR

By the same author

'Let Wonder Seem Familiar': Endings in Shakespeare's Romance Endings (London: Athlone Press, 1985).
Innocent Victims: Poetic Injustice in Shakespearean Tragedy (second edition, London: Athlone Press, 1986).
Keats as a Reader of Shakespeare (London, Athlone Press, 1987).
Furphy's Shakespeare (Nedlands: Centre for Studies in Australian Literature, 1989).

Edited with Graham McGregor
The Art of Listening (London: Routledge, 1986).
Reception and Response (London: Routledge, 1990).

Twayne's New Critical
Introductions to Shakespeare

THE MERRY WIVES OF WINDSOR

R. S. White

Professor of English,
University of Western Australia

Twayne Publishers, Boston
A Division of G. K. Hall & Co.

Published in the United States by Twayne Publishers
A Division of G. K. Hall & Co.
70 Lincoln Street
Boston, Massachusetts 02111

Published simultaneously in Great Britain by
Harvester Wheatsheaf
66 Wood Lane End, Hemel Hempstead
Hertfordshire HP2 4RG
A division of
Simon & Schuster International Group

Twayne's New Critical Introductions to Shakespeare, no. 11

Library of Congress Cataloging–in–Publication Data

White, R. S., 1948–
    The merry wives of Windsor / R.S. White.
        p.   cm. — (Twayne's new critical introductions to Shakespeare
    : v. 11)
    includes bibliographical references and index.
    ISBN 0–8057–8722–4. — ISBN 0–8057–8723–2 (pbk.)
    1. Shakespeare, William, 1564–1616. Merry wives of Windsor.
I. Shakespeare, William, 1584–1616. Merry wives of Windsor.
II. Title.   III. Series.
PR2826.W47   1991
822.3'3--dc20   91-13111
                                                                                      CIP

Titles in the Series

General Editor's Preface

The *New Critical Introductions to Shakespeare* series will include studies of all Shakespeare's plays, together with two volumes on the non-dramatic verse, and is designed to offer a challenge to all students of Shakespeare.

Each volume will be brief enough to read in an evening, but long enough to avoid those constraints which are inevitable in articles and short essays. Each contributor will develop a sustained critical reading of the play in question, which addresses those difficulties and critical disagreements which each play has generated.

Different plays present different problems, different challenges and excitements. In isolating these, each volume will present a preliminary survey of the play's stage history and critical reception. The volumes then provide a more extended discussion of these matters in the main text, and of matters relating to genre, textual problems and the use of source material, or to historical and theoretical issues. But here, rather than setting a row of dragons at the gate, we have assumed that 'background' should figure only as it emerges into a critical foreground; part of the critical endeavour is to establish, and sift, those issues which seem most pressing.

So, for example, when Shakespeare determined that *his*

Othello and Desdemona should have no time to live together, or that Cordelia dies while Hermione survives, his deliberate departures from his source material have a critical significance which is often blurred, when discussed in the context of lengthily detailed surveys of 'the sources'. Alternatively, plays like *The Merchant of Venice* or *Measure for Measure* show Shakespeare welding together different 'stories' from quite different sources, so that their relation to each other becomes a matter for critical debate. And Shakespeare's dramatic practice poses different critical questions when we ask – or if we ask: few do – why particular characters in a poetic drama speak only in verse or only in prose; or when we try to engage with those recent, dauntingly specialised and controversial textual studies which set out to establish the evidence for authorial revisions or joint authorship. We all read *King Lear* and *Macbeth*, but we are not all textual critics; nor are textual critics always able to show where their arguments have critical consequences which concern us all.

Just as we are not all textual critics, we are not all linguists, cultural anthropologists, psychoanalysts or New Historicists. The diversity of contemporary approaches to Shakespeare is unprecedented, enriching, bewildering. One aim of this series is to represent what is illuminating in this diversity. As the hastiest glance through the list of contributors will confirm, the series does not attempt to 'reread' Shakespeare by placing an ideological grid over the text and reporting on whatever shows through. Nor would the series' contributors always agree with each other's arguments, or premises; but each has been invited to develop a sustained critical argument which will also provide its own critical and historical context – by taking account of those issues which have perplexed or divided audiences, readers, and critics past and present.

Graham Bradshaw

Contents

Preface

This book differs from some other 'critical introductions' in that it does not proceed chronologically through the play. Rather, it presents a series of relatively self-sufficient essays on different aspects of *The Merry Wives of Windsor* and different ways in which it can be, and has been, interpreted. At the same time, I hope that a unified argument runs through the book. It is unavoidable that there will be some overlaps and repetitions, since the various issues impinge on each other. The perspective, drawing on the word 'New' in the series title, is one that takes account of recent developments in literary criticism, which is incorporating forms of analysis taken from such areas as linguistics, historical contextualisation, feminism and gender studies, economics and Marxism. At the same time, I have tried not to overload the play with theoretical concerns, nor even to speak theoretically, but to concentrate on the action and words of the play. Renaissance writers saw it as their duty to 'teach and delight', and there was about equal concentration on these two aims. We have until recently tended to exclude the 'teaching' function from literary studies, preferring to see works of literature and art as a wonderful 'bonus' designed to enhance our leisure hours and distract us with 'timeless truths' from the world we live in. The furore caused by the appearance of Tom Paulin's *Faber Book of Political Poetry* proved that many people see politics and poetry as antithetical to each other. Such a position would have puzzled the Renaissance writer and theorist. Recent literary theory is retrieving the political and moral dimensions in literature and art, and because this task is so important its exponents have sometimes risked losing the 'delight'. And yet *The Merry Wives of Windsor* is a delight to read and to see performed, and it is this impression which criticism should at least attempt to convey.

Acknowledgements

I have enjoyed writing this book. For this I should mainly thank Shakespeare, but there have been others apart from the only begetter: Graham Bradshaw for inviting me to write it and for his valuable suggestions, Jackie Jones for her inspirational efficiency, those who listened to operas at the New Norcia Humanities Symposium, and Jane Whiteley for her warmhearted help and support. I have written here as an enthusiast speaking unashamedly to other enthusiasts, and I must thank several generations of students at the Universities of Newcastle upon Tyne and Western Australia for fostering and protecting my confidence to do so. I dedicate the book to my colleague, mentor and friend, Ernst Honigmann, holding my breath in the hope that he will enjoy it.

There is more life and reality in the first act of *The Merry Wives of Windsor* alone than in all German literature.

Engels to Marx, 10 December 1873

Introduction

A NOTE ON THE TEXTS

A few words need to be said at the outset about the text itself. We are inclined to regard 'the text' of a play by Shakespeare as something fixed, immutable, and almost sacred in its integrity. Sometimes we give it biblical treatment by praising a reading or a performance as 'faithful' or even authorised, and deriding one that 'distorts the text'. The assumptions behind such statements are indefensible. Nothing is more unstable and negotiable in literary matters than a text of a Renaissance play. Between the writing of a script and the performance of a play on the Elizabethan stage lay as many transformations as exist today between the writing and the performance of a film or television screenplay. Many people intervened along the way, and it is necessary to speak of the journey towards production as a process which is at no one point complete or fixed. A playtext in manuscript has always been assumed to be a provisional starting-point, and in rehearsal, especially when the dramatist is involved, many changes are bound to be made. Even from performance to performance there are changes which are not recorded in a 'text' but which depend instead on the dynamics of the theatre and its audiences.

Similarly, from reading to reading of a play one individual will find new significances, new dimensions, new 'readings'. Even in dealing with a written record there is no final stability. No printed text of a play by Shakespeare was, to our knowledge, authorised and approved for publication by him. During a dramatist's lifetime, the acting company which produced his plays had a vested interest in preventing publication, since, unrestricted by copyright laws, other companies could steal situations, lines and characters without restraint. If scripts were published, it was as likely as not that they were 'pirated', printed without the permission or collaboration of the writer or dramatic company. The first 'Collected Works' of Shakespeare, what is known as the *First Folio*, was published in 1623, seven years after his death, by friends who almost certainly did not have access in every case to the words Shakespeare would have preferred to see in print. In every case where an earlier (Quarto) edition exists, the Folio differs from it in significant ways which sometimes seem aesthetically superior and sometimes inferior. Editors are now arguing that Shakespeare himself revised his plays, either because of the demands of differing performing contexts, or changing censorship laws. Furthermore, since Shakespeare's time we have seen the growth of a whole industry of Shakespeare editing, which results in a host of differences of opinion between editors. This means that every edition of *The Merry Wives of Windsor* which we can lay our hands on will have differences from others. There is no such thing as a final, stable, sanctified text of 'The Play'.

Such dizzying relativity even at the basic level of text may seem dismaying at first, but the implications for a critic and reader are healthy. If the text exists in a state of plural potential, then criticism is licensed also in presenting many interpretations (no single one being the only 'correct' version), in line with the many responses readers and audiences have had to the play. Even a single interpretation, especially a convincing one, can hold in suspension many different options which may be attended to or discarded by readers according to their predilections. Criticism can be a magnificently republican democracy instead of an authoritarian dictatorship by those who claim a single, immutable 'truth'.

Although *The Merry Wives of Windsor* does not pose especially difficult textual problems, the 'transmission' of the text of even this play reinforces the point that there are variant readings. The play may have been first performed as early as 1597 (though there is great dispute even about this), but no written record exists of the text used on that occasion. The first we find of it in published form is in a book (called a Quarto because of its size) which appeared in 1602, and already the title-page indicates that the play 'hath been divers times acted by the Right Honourable my Lord Chamberlain's Servants, both before her majesty and elsewhere'. Who knows what changes occurred in a period of perhaps five years of its 'divers' performances? Moreover, the Quarto text is regarded as somewhat suspect because it is very short in comparison with the later edition. Since all the scenes in which Falstaff and the Host appear seem consistent in detail and dramatic coherence, whilst other parts are clearly defective, it has been surmised that the actors who played these two characters dictated to the publisher's scribe what they could remember of the play (making it a 'memorial reconstruction'). There is some justification for this explanation because we know that each actor was issued only with the script for his own part(s) – a means by which the theatrical company tried to safeguard against the 'industrial espionage' of a play being given to a rival company *in toto*. But we do not know for sure if this is the explanation, and an equally possible line of reasoning would say that Shakespeare rewrote his plays, each time adding layers of richness and attentiveness to detail, layer upon layer. Most living writers will confirm such a possibility in the process of composition. The Quarto text was republished in 1619. The next edition was the 1623 Folio (again named because of the size of the book), the collection of almost all Shakespeare's plays compiled by his friends

Heminge and Condell, who may have had access to some kind of Shakespearian original. The text of *The Merry Wives* is almost twice as long, and it seems more generally trustworthy in detail. It forms the basis for modern editions, although in some details the Quarto is still preferred. Again, where exactly this text came from is shrouded in doubt, especially since it appeared more than twenty years after the play's first production. Nowadays, where there are significant differences between a Quarto and the Folio, there is a tendency to argue that the second is a revision of the former, sometimes amounting to a new play (as in the case of *King Lear*). The argument has not been put for *The Merry Wives* but if this line were followed up it could give fascinating evidence of how Shakespeare wrote, revised and changed his plays. Certainly, some things have been changed to conform to ever-stricter censorship laws about the use of oaths on the Jacobean stage. All subsequent editors have used the Folio as the basis of their task in establishing a 'complete' text, using some parts of the Quarto which seem 'authentic'. Right down the centuries you will find that all editors have made different choices, so that no two editions are the same. Even today, if you examine texts by different editors (say the New Penguin, the Arden, the Signet, the Alexander text and the new Oxford *Complete Works*), you will find dozens of variants, usually minor but *in toto* confirming the conclusion that no matter how many experts you collect they will never come up with an agreed, 'perfect' text. There are always many discrepancies in punctuation, for example, because Elizabethan punctuation was fairly arbitrary and was usually supplied by the publisher rather than the author. Even today, punctuation is more personal and less subject to rules than most people admit. While punctuation does not seem of much importance, it can sometimes affect the meaning. In this book, incidentally, the text quoted from is the New Penguin edition, edited by G. R. Hibbard, for no special reasons except that it is cheap, reliable and easy to read.

There is even some evidence that Shakespeare himself

could not have regarded any of the texts available as
complete, for even in the earliest ones there is a 'loose end' in
the plot which he would certainly have tied up. It seems to
have been a kind of 'false start' in the plot which again gives
us a unique glimpse into his mode of composition. You will
find some references to a strand of the story which is never
integrated. At II. i. 88–90 Mistress Page plans, as part of the
revenge on Falstaff, that he be persuaded to pawn his horses
to the Host of the Garter Inn. Whatever happens to this
trick we never hear, but the horses surface later as part of a
plot to deceive the Host himself. In the apparently irrelevant
little scene IV. iii Bardolph requests three horses from the
Host to give to visiting Germans who are staying at the Inn
apparently at the command of a mysterious German duke.
The Host agrees to give the horses but at an exorbitant price
('I'll make them pay. I'll sauce them'). The Host is also told
he will meet the Duke the next day, and although suspicious
because of the clandestine nature of the Duke's movements,
he agrees to the plan. In a following scene (IV. v. 59–75) the
Host is informed that the three Germans have ridden off with
his horses, '. . . set spurs and away, like three German devils,
three Doctor Faustuses' (IV. v. 64). The Host wants to
believe that 'Germans are honest men' and that they have
simply ridden off to meet the Duke, but he is immediately
informed by Evans that there are three German 'cozeners'
(thieves) who have already robbed all the hosts in the area of
horses and money. Caius then informs the Host that the
Duke of Germany does not exist. The Host rushes off,
setting up a hue and cry, lamenting that he is ruined. All this
is rather puzzling, since the connections between the
episode, the main plot and Falstaff's horses are problematical. Since it is Evans and Caius who bring the news, we
presume they are taking revenge on the Host for leading
them apart from each other and thus aborting the duel, but it
all seems redundant. Arguments can be made, but they are
strained, and many critics have been thrown back on the
admirable evasion of suspecting topical reference. All we
can conclude is either that Shakespeare at some stage had

another strand of the plot in mind which he has not brought fully into being, or that the episode is complete in itself but not fully integrated with the rest. Again, the spectre of an authorised text, complete and perfect, eludes us.

CRITICAL RECEPTION

The same can be said about critical interpretations of the play. None has been, or ever will be, formulated to meet the universal satisfaction of all readers at all times. Partly this is because each reader has different centres of interest from all others, and even one will have different ideas on each reading. Partly, also, every reader is predisposed by the historical period and social environment in which he or she lives towards asking individual questions and finding personal solutions. We can never fully know in what ways we are restricted or liberated, consciously and unconsciously, by the climate of opinion in which we live – but that we *are* conditioned in some ways is certain. Age, gender, social class, political assumptions, occupation and field of expertise will all have some influence on the meanings we 'discover' (or perhaps 'read into') literature, and this is equally true whether a critic claims to be presenting a 'universal truth' or a definably 'contemporary' interpretation. As a simple example, even the very word 'Windsor' has connoted many different things to different people, and it will continue to do so. I must admit that I take these statements to be self-evidently true, but since they will be regarded as controversial by some, I hope to substantiate them with reference to the history of criticism of *The Merry Wives of Windsor*. (Full details of critical works mentioned are given in the Bibliography at the end of the book.)

Samuel Pepys was a hard-headed, practical man of business whose greatest contribution, as a civil servant, was to place the British Navy on an efficient footing. It might be too easy to say that such a man was not temperamentally fitted to appreciate finer sentiments of either comedy or love, and yet judging from his comments on some of Shakespeare's plays this seems to be the case. He is like Polonius in his attitude to plays, proclaiming his expert knowledge but crass in his tastes. Certainly, he was not disposed to see much good in *The Merry Wives*, for he wrote in his Diary on 5 December 1660:

> I dined at home, and after dinner I went to the new Theatre and there I saw 'The Merry Wives of Windsor' acted, the humours of the country gentleman [Shallow] and the French doctor very well done, but the rest very poorly, and Sir J. Falstaffe as bad as any.

(It might be possible to exonerate him if we think he is speaking of the production rather than the play itself, but for Pepys the two may well have been synonymous.) John Dryden, a man of his time in accepting the need for plays to observe certain rules of decorum, in 1679 praised *The Merry Wives* as one of the few plays by Shakespeare excelling in 'the mechanic beauties of the plot, which are the observation of the three Unities, Time, Place and Action . . .'. This was supremely important in the judgement of writers of the eighteenth century (who willingly 'corrected' Shakespeare's plays by rewriting them) but is now of virtually no interest.

John Dennis in 1702 set the course for the next 250 years of commentary by claiming knowledge that the play was written at the command of Queen Elizabeth who 'commanded it to be finished in fourteen days'. Nicholas Rowe in 1709 embellished the tradition by saying that the Queen specifically asked to see Falstaff 'in Love':

> She was so well pleas'd with that admirable Character of *Falstaff*, in the two Parts of *Henry the Fourth*, that she commanded him to continue it for one Play more, and to shew him in Love. This is said to be the Occasion of his

Writing *The Merry Wives of Windsor*. How well she was obey'd the Play it self is an admirable Proof.

A tradition which surfaces more than a century after the writing of the play is fairly tenuous, and yet it became, instead, tenacious, since subsequent critics down to the present day felt they had to address it. A consequence is that the one character is centralised at the expense of the design as a whole, and in such an intricately crafted plot this is a great risk. Moreover, because the uniform opinion was that the character Falstaff lacked the vitality he had shown in the *Henry IV* plays, the whole play was also considered weak and defective. Samuel Johnson in 1773 acutely diagnosed why Falstaff could never be shown 'in Love' with felicitous results:

> Falstaff could not love, but by ceasing to be Falstaff. He could only counterfeit love, and his professions could be prompted, not by the hope of pleasure, but of money.

We should remember that Falstaff appears in other plays by Shakespeare, *1 Henry IV*, *2 Henry IV* and *Henry V*, and it is partly knowledge of these plays which informs Johnson's judgement. But even without this background, it is a sharp observation upon the Falstaff of *The Merry Wives*, and one which could have led on to an interesting account of the play as a whole. Johnson had interesting things to say about 'the effect of language distorted and depraved by provincial or foreign pronunciation' (a special interest of the man who wrote one of the first dictionaries of English), and he praised the 'variety and number of the personages'. But guided by his neoclassical preconceptions he concludes that the play is 'deficient', lacking 'general power'. With an impenetrable ambiguity, he observes that the play is one which perhaps 'never yet had reader or spectator, who did not think it too soon at an end'. The negatives in this sentence make it difficult to say whether Johnson is admiring the play or being drily critical.

The great Romantic critic S. T. Coleridge found more to his

taste in an 'exceedingly diverting' comedy, and the romantic ideas of his own age may well have led him to appreciate the 'delightful' women (the nineteenth century as a whole idealised Shakespeare's women), and also, interestingly, to note the power of the jealousy theme: 'Ford's jealousy is of too serious a complexion for the rest of the play' (again, early nineteenth-century critics were fascinated by *Othello* and by extreme psychological states). William Hazlitt, Coleridge's contemporary, while noting the 'amusing' quality of *The Merry Wives* is almost completely distracted by what he regards as the failure of Falstaff. Some of his asides are interesting. He too notices the jealousy of Ford, and goes so far as to say it is 'the main spring of the comic incidents', considering it 'certainly very well managed'. Rather oddly, he dismisses Page as 'somewhat uxorious in his disposition' though it is difficult to see why Page's love of his wife should be a fault: perhaps Hazlitt, a realist rather than a romantic at heart, felt that Page's unquestioning trust is exaggerated. (Hazlitt's own marriage was unhappy.) The poet John Keats, who wrote in a letter 'I look upon fine Phrases like a Lover', clearly found many such phrases when he read the play, since his edition of the text is considerably marked, and he also laced his letters in jocular fashion with snatches of quotations and echoes from *The Merry Wives*.

During the late nineteenth century some of the contemporary debates about class, generated by Karl Marx and the rise of the labour movement in Britain, even crept into the ivory tower of criticism, usually in the form of a rather covert defence of the middle class. Hence we find F. S. Boas in 1896 praising the play's overall construction, its 'capital situations' and 'breezy' movement, and he rather cleverly links these delights of the play not only with the legend of Elizabeth's intervention but also with the virtues of the middle class:

> It deals purely with *bourgeois* life, and critics have seen in this an additional evidence that it was prepared for the special benefit of Elizabeth and her train, who would

relish this vigorous sketch of middle-class society, with its manners and morals so entirely at variance with those of a refined and dissolute court.

Why Elizabeth should wish to see her own class and court betrayed in the way implied by Boas is not clear. The opening sentence of a monumental book by E. K. Chambers, *William Shakespeare*, published in 1930, is 'William Shakespeare was born of burgess folk, not unlike those whom he depicts in *The Merry Wives of Windsor*'. ('Burgess' is bourgeois anglicised.) G. K. Hunter, in an illuminating essay, has explored the 'bourgeois' issues in the play, comparing it with the contemporary play by Dekker, *The Shoemaker's Holiday*. While we need not challenge this emphasis, we should be aware of it as a modern construction owing much to economic analysis of classes carried out over the last hundred or so years.

The twentieth century has not produced a univocal, consistent critical approach to *The Merry Wives*, but it has opened up various paths. Critics such as John Russell Brown and John Dover Wilson inadvertently display the legacy of the 'ironist' school of modernist poetry by lamenting the fact that so many characters are subjected to gross ridicule (modernist poets like Eliot and Pound feared exposure of one's vulnerabilities, and preferred modes that had a protective layer of irony – something largely lacking in the broad effects of *The Merry Wives*). This view is related to the most common modern approach, which is to see the play not as revealing depths of characterisation of thematic interest, but largely in terms of its plot. Accordingly, it has been dismissed as mere farce or fondly celebrated for its controlled, intricate plotting. Leo Salingar is one who has sympathetically analysed the play from the point of view of its craftsmanlike construction, linking it with conventions Shakespeare could have found in Italian comedy.

Some writers turned their backs altogether on evaluative criticism, preferring rather to explore the historical circumstances of the play's composition, a line of approach which has in fact led to a fruitful resurrection of the historical method of criticism under the blazon of 'New Historicism'. One could 'contextualise' *The Merry Wives* by making reference to Elizabethan marriage mores and the place of women, so far as these issues can be known from a twentieth-century vantage point. However, it may be indicative of the lack of genuine *critical* interest taken in the play by professional critics that before the present work, the only book-length accounts of *The Merry Wives of Windsor* have been historical in the much narrower sense of considering the play's 'occasion', and they contain very little interpretation as such. These are the books by Hotson, Green, and Roberts.

An idea which took root in the 1950s, 1960s and 1970s was connected with the rise of an interest in 'cultural anthropology', the linking up of apparently traditional social rituals with their expression in literature. The two greatest critics in this school were Northrop Frye and C. L. Barber, and they have had a host of followers. Barber did not write on the play, but it would fit very well his theory of 'festive comedy' as a social catharsis, and Frye in 1948 found at least one very pregnant idea of his in *The Merry Wives*:

> In *The Merry Wives of Windsor* there is an elaborate ritual of the defeat of winter, known to folklorists as 'carrying out Death,' of which Falstaff is the victim: and Falstaff must have felt that, after being thrown into the water, dressed up as a witch and beaten out of a house with curses, and finally supplied with a beast's head and singed with candles while he said, 'Divide me like a brib'd buck, each a haunch' (v. v. 24), he had done about all that could reasonably be asked of any fertility spirit.

Falstaff becomes a classic 'scapegoat' figure, whose expulsion preludes the regeneration of the social order. This whole approach has come in for considerable criticism and revision in the 1970s and 1980s, and on the particular subject of *The Merry Wives* Anne Barton in 1985 trenchantly argued that the whole idea of ritual renewal is quite inappropriate to an understanding of a play which is rooted in social comedy rather than myth or ritual. Her attitude, again, can be linked with the close analysis of social interactions associated with the rise of sociology in the 1980s, and which in other hands has led to a school of criticism which calls itself 'cultural materialism'. A prevailing way of categorising the play is as 'citizen comedy', which stresses the social and economic aspects to the detriment of the romantic and ritualistic. But ideas will always find some supporters even when their day seems to have passed. An interest related to Frye's is developed by William Carroll in a book on 'metamorphosis' which takes some of its leading ideas from sixteenth-century ideas of witchcraft. Ruth Nevo in *Comic Transformation in Shakespeare* follows up Frye's interest in classical Old and New comedy and their roots in ritual, while Jeanne Addison Roberts goes so far as to argue that the 'dis-horning' of 'Fallstaff' is a symbolic castration ritual. Another general modern interest relating to pagan ritual has been the whole subject of revenge, and Linda M. Anderson has looked in detail at how the plot structure of revenge works in comedy. Her chapter on *The Merry Wives* is one of the most convincing in her book.

Bertrand Evans in 1960 pioneered a kind of criticism that is sophisticated in dealing with the ways in which plays work as theatrical artefacts, when he developed the idea of 'discrepant awareness' at work in the plays. He pointed out that there is considerable dramatic significance in the fact that there are hierarchies of knowledge among characters, and that subtle ironies stem from the playwright's exploitation of these discrepancies. So thorough is Evans in unravelling the ironies of awareness in *The Merry Wives* that it is difficult to see how anybody could go much further along this line.

One of the most recent advances in literary criticism has come from the rise of the feminist movement in the 1970s and its consolidation in the 1980s. A much more hard-headed approach to the subject of Shakespeare's depiction of women in social situations has replaced the Victorian sentimentality. Muriel Bradbrook spoke in 1968 of 'the old traditional triumph of the women's league' in the play and Jeanne Addison Roberts in 1970 looked in detail at how Mistress Ford and Mistress Page act as 'defenders of the social order' restoring a hopeful vision. Marilyn French, in a book published in 1981, sees the society of Windsor as 'masculine' in its preoccupation with property and the threat to property posed by strangers: 'The major themes of the play are the cornerstones of bourgeois life: possession of property, possession of women, and fear of theft.' Taken a little further, this line of approach can easily turn into a critique of Shakespeare's own assumptions about what underpins an orderly or stable society – there is a distinct possibility that the women are reinforcing male complacencies about marriage and property, missing an opportunity radically to undermine the men's proprietorial assumptions. Such a critical approach has been taken by Peter Erickson who concludes that in the play female power is acknowledged but only as a threat to men and not as a progressive subversiveness of 'a patriarchally inflected framework'. Feminists argue among themselves on the point of Shakespeare's progressive or reactionary assumptions. Linda Woodbridge in her splendid book *Women and the English Renaissance: Literature and the nature of womankind, 1540–1620* makes few references to *The Merry Wives* but she provides a wealth of information, both historical and literary, which helps us to set the play in its context and avoid an anachronistic reading. Marilyn French sees the women in *The Merry Wives* as radical threats to male supremacy, but Sandra Clark, while noting their 'corrective' influence, argues that the women 'at the same time . . . share fully in the men's attitudes towards property and self-preservation'. The terms of this argument demonstrate that even readers who share similar principles and interests may come to diametrically opposite conclusions about a play like

The Merry Wives of Windsor. In the circumstances, I claim for my own approach an openness which I hope will lead others into their own thoughts and their own readings.

STAGE HISTORY

Readers of this book may by now be forgiven for thinking that Shakespeare experts are marked by *not* knowing much about Shakespeare. This is not entirely fair, since in every intellectual field it is better to be cautiously aware of the limitations on our knowledge than simply to proclaim assertions based on our 'authority'. Furthermore it is being acknowledged in areas as diverse as physics, chemistry and history that the observer (whether scientist or critic) will inevitably be affecting the object of enquiry simply by asking certain questions based on preconceived and often unexamined assumptions. Sometimes it is better even for experts to admit ignorance and, at best, to guide readers into the realms of the possible. All this comes by way of confession that we know *nothing* about the first stage performances of *The Merry Wives*.

Of course, there is much speculation which often masquerades as 'fact'. One school, represented most cogently by Leslie Hotson, William Green and Jeanne Roberts, and implicitly accepted by Peter Erickson, builds upon the tradition that Shakespeare wrote the play at the invitation of Queen Elizabeth. Rather than latching on to the anecdotal idea that she wanted to see Falstaff in love, however, they detect the particular quality of an 'occasional' play – a play written for a specific occasion. Because the play is set in Windsor and features prominently the Garter Inn, these writers discover an appropriate occasion, the investment of the Order of the Garter upon George Carey, Lord Hunsdon (patron of Shakespeare's company) on St George's Day (23 April) 1597 at the Garter Feast held at Whitehall Palace in Westminster. In the absence of any facts whatsoever, this seems a brilliant speculation that ought to settle the matter. However, J. M. Nosworthy and G. R. Hibbard ungratefully cast some cold water on the theory, and they favour a date which would put the play conclusively after the perform- ance of both parts of *Henry IV* and *Henry V*, that is, in 1599 or later. There is a case for putting it after *2 Henry IV* (which *may* have been written in 1598) since that play contains Justice Shallow, Nym and Pistol, but before *Henry V* because in the last play Pistol is married to Mistress Quickly (an event anticipated in *The Merry Wives* at II. ii. 131–4). This argument, however, is premised on assumptions about consistent Shakespearian characterisation that may be ques- tioned. Mistress Quickly, as Hostess of the Boar's Head Tavern in London in the Henry plays, need not be the same 'character' who bears the name in *The Merry Wives*. The same applies to Justice Shallow who, in *2 Henry IV*, while bearing a resemblance in speech patterns to the Shallow of *The Merry Wives*, appears as Justice in Gloucestershire rather than Windsor. There is no necessary reason why Shakespeare should not invent Falstaff's raffish companions for *The Merry Wives* and then take them on the recruiting mission in *2 Henry IV*. Equally, it cannot be completely ruled out that Shakespeare invented the whole set of charac- ters, including Falstaff, in *The Merry Wives* and that the Henry plays, extending and enriching the possibilities of them, are the product of one pregnant line when Page says of Fenton that 'He kept company with the wild Prince and Poins' (III. ii. 66). The 'wild Prince' of course is Hal in *1 Henry IV* and the first part of *2 Henry IV*, tamed into the responsibility of kingship in *Henry V*. Shakespeare may well have thought Fenton too dull to resurrect, while spotting the enormous potential for pitting Falstaff against the wild Prince. On the other hand, it is tempting to think that the ripely nostalgic, pastoral scenes in Gloucestershire (III. ii and v. i) in *2 Henry IV* were the creative inspiration for the provincial setting and feel of *The Merry Wives*. All we can conclude is that no theory need compel acceptance and none tells us anything definite about the first stage performance of *The Merry Wives*. Nor does the speculation, based on some slender textual evidence, that Shakespeare was throughout making satirical reference to the living family of the Cobhams, whose ancestor was Falstaff (under the name of Oldcastle) and who numbered among their ranks a Brooke. All we really know is what the title-page to the Quarto tells us. By 1602 the play 'hath been divers times acted by the Right Honourable my Lord Chamberlain's Servants [Shakespeare's company], both before her majesty and elsewhere'.

The history of its subsequent stage performances is less misty and also less controversial. Apart from Pepys' sour comment in 1660, *The Merry Wives* has elicited little adverse comment on its theatrical realisations. This is in marked contrast to the churlish chorus of literary critics over the centuries who keep reminding us of its defects. James I was at a performance in 1604 at the royal palace of Whitehall. Charles I took his queen to a staging at the Cockpit Theatre in 1638. The date of Pepys' comment (December 1660) is evidence that the play was highly enough regarded to be among the vanguard of plays to be revived after the theatres reopened on the Restoration of the monarchy in that year. Hazlitt, a great theatre critic, was satisfied with the play in performance and his strictures against it were based simply on the fact that he had a different set of expectations about Falstaff. As we shall see, the play was a great favourite for translation into opera in the eighteenth and nineteenth centuries and even by Vaughan Williams in the twentieth. Arthur Sullivan (of Gilbert and Sullivan fame, but before he had met his future collaborator) liked it enough to write a musical score to the play in 1874 which was played at the Gaiety Theatre in London and again in 1889 at the Haymarket. The play also had the distinction of inspiring an epic painting in 1840, David Scott's 'Queen Elizabeth Viewing the Performance of the "Merry Wives of Windsor" in the Globe Theatre' which was hung at the Royal Academy summer exhibition.

The play has had regular, well-received revivals in the

latter half of the twentieth century. The Royal Shakespeare Company played it in 1968, 1975, 1979 and 1985, among other occasions. It was played at the Shakespeare Festival at Stratford, Ontario in 1982 and again in 1990, and has been to the People's Republic of China in the 1980s in a joint American and Chinese production. These are only a few of the many revivals, none of which seems to have failed with audiences.

The temporal transportability of *The Merry Wives* is shown in a different way by the fact that Bill Alexander, Associate Director of the Royal Shakespeare Company in the 1980s, chose to set it in the late 1950s. In an interview with Ralph Berry published in Berry's *On Directing Shakespeare* he justified the decision by saying that the play demanded a very strong sense of *milieu* which could be evoked for an audience of the 1980s by setting it in 'the confident, late-Fifties' world, a world that was putting the war and authority behind it . . . [when] the bourgeoisie was rich and confident'. A revealing review of the production, illustrated with photographs and written by Nicholas Shrimpton, can be found in *Shakespeare Survey* 39 (1987), pp. 196–9. Arguments have also been made that the play is so specifically rooted in Elizabeth I's England of the 1590s that it should be set then. Again, a director would have the sanction of a different authority in using a late medieval setting, for the reference to Prince Hal means it was historically set in that period. It seems to 'work' whenever it is located, and demands only some consistency of direction and enthusiastic acting.

The play has been 'translated' into various different media. Leaving aside its operatic adaptations which will be examined later in the book, it was made into a black and white, silent film in the United States in 1910, and then again in Germany in 1917 as *Die Lustigen Weiber von Windsor*. I have not seen either of these, but the second must have had a very curious existence, if it was made in Germany towards the end of the First World War when the country was impoverished and torn. Then in 1952 and shortly after in 1955

The Merry Wives was made into different television plays by the BBC in Britain. In 1982 the BBC, in collaboration with Time-Life TV, filmed the play as part of its complete Shakespeare series. It starred Richard Griffiths as Falstaff, Prunella Scales as Mistress Page, Judy Davis as Mistress Ford and Ben Kingsley as Ford.

The Merry Wives of Windsor is justly entrenched in the amateur repertoire because it utilises a large cast without requiring a 'star' actor (even Falstaff's role is manageable), and because of its sheer, extroverted comedy. The scene of Falstaff's incarceration in the buck-basket to the amusement of the women and the ignorant fury of Ford is among the greatest of Shakespeare's orchestrated, comic climaxes. The whole atmosphere of Windsor which I shall try to follow in analysis is eccentric but cohesive, evoking a myth of 'merry England' which has never existed but owes its imaginative attractiveness to Shakespeare's own myth-making powers.

All this is evidence of a thoroughly successful, stageworthy play, and so much we would expect from its craftsmanlike, expert splicing of complex, comic plots, and its gallery of unique characters. There is enough reason to consider the play as one worthy of serious and sympathetic study.

· 1 ·

The Town of Windsor

It is dangerous, and perhaps impossible, to claim that any work of literature or art is 'realistic'. All that art can give us is a model of a possible world, and we as spectators locate ourselves either close to or distant from that world. The work of Ernst Gombrich and John Berger in the field of pictorial art, and the developing ideas of semioticians, prove that art works through conventions and codes which we as viewers and readers feel either comfortable with or uneasy in decoding. Moreover, as 'metatheatrical' critics (J. L. Calderwood is the main exponent) have insistently shown, Shakespeare in particular rarely allows us to forget that we are watching (or reading) a stage play rather than observing what pretends to be unmediated 'reality'. Such theatrical consciousness is at work in this play. On several occasions characters use theatrical terms when speaking of their own activities:

Misress Ford.	Mistress Page, remember you your cue.
Mistress Page.	I warrant thee; if I do not act it, hiss me.
	(III. iii. 34–5)
Falstaff.	. . . after we had embraced, kissed, protested, and, as it were, spoken the prologue of our comedy . . .
	(III. v. 68–9)

The scene in the Forest at the end is presented as a masque by characters who are very conscious of the fictive roles they play. The effects of such 'metatheatrical' aspects of presentation can be very problematical (as in *Hamlet*) and it may even be an open question as to whether the effect is to distance us from the action or, paradoxically, to make us feel it is more naturalistic. Comments such as Mistress Page's can simultaneously make us aware that we are in a theatre watching actors and contribute to the overall sense that the play itself has its distinctive, internally consistent 'possible world' with its own norms of what is real and what is not.

In terms of the 'possible worlds' given to us by Shakespeare in his plays, some are either more or less remote from what we recognise as a specific 'locality' with its own ethos within which we can assume a proximity to a 'realistic' setting. His comedies generally give us never-never lands like the dreamy Illyria, the literary Forest of Arden (or Ardennes, as the New Oxford Shakespeare insists), the romantic Belmont or the commercially-minded and vindictive Venice, the madcap forest outside Athens. Such settings take us away from any recognisable day-by-day existence. There is a stratum of such 'romantic' conventions in *The Merry Wives* found in the wooing of Anne Page, the comic disguises of Falstaff as the fat lady of Brainford, of Mistress Quickly as the Fairy Queen, of Slender and Doctor Caius, Anne and Fenton, and indeed all characters except Falstaff in the last scene. In this scene we even have a forest which has its transformative magic, able to bring couples together (and back together, like the Fords).

However, compared with full-blooded romantic comedy, Windsor in our play seems solidly rooted in its specified town planning, its diurnal activities, its local customs. It is, after all, English (the only comedy Shakespeare set in England), and it is a geographically precise location whose central landmark, the pub called the Garter Inn, still exists. The play is also the one and only example by Shakespeare of Citizen Comedy, a genre which was popular in the early seventeenth century, showing the middle class involved to a large extent in believable commercial transactions as well as love, rather than the aristocratic, fantasy milieu of romantic comedy. There may even be a little joke by Shakespeare in all this, since by mentioning Windsor he may have raised audience expectations about seeing the private life of the court, since the town is where the Royal Palace was (and still is), only to disappoint them by scrupulously not showing court life. This is not, however, to say that what Shakespeare does with the town of Windsor is necessarily 'realistic', and still less is it to say that the characters are 'real', for a more eccentric lot could hardly be imagined. The play is certainly not in the mould of 'social realism' as the term is understood today, and the plot is too elaborately crafted in multi-layered fashion to be a 'slice of life'.

No matter how we need to qualify the statement, it is possible to talk about the Windsor of the play as a small, self-sufficient society which is 'characterised' by local references. Early on we get chatter about town life which is inconsequential to the plot but is important in building up a social setting. Mr Page thanks Justice Shallow for a gift of venison, Shallow regrets it is not of the top quality (it was badly killed, perhaps by Falstaff), and he enquires after Mistress Page's health. Slender indulges in gentle banter about Shallow's greyhound which is rumoured to have lost a race at a meeting in the Cotswolds. And then the dialogue returns to the matter in hand, the troubles caused by Falstaff. There are neighbourly meals, one to be held before a sea-coal fire (sea-coal was gathered at Newcastle upon Tyne and Sunderland and shipped down to the south, thus acquiring something of a status symbol for its price and superior quality). One meal concludes with pippin apples and cheese. When dogs bark, Slender surmises that there are bears in town and he recalls seeing the famous London bear Sackerson 'loose twenty times' (I. i. 274). This detail partly fixes Slender as one who enjoys male, violent pursuits (he has bruised his shin at fencing with a sword and dagger, revels in bear-baiting, and will later collude in a duel), and it also helps to characterise the township's men in general.

Geographical references are often particularised. John and Robert, Ford's servants, must take the laundry-basket 'among the whitsters in Datchet Mead, and there empty it in the muddy ditch close by the Thames side' (III. iii. 14–15). The fat woman impersonated by Falstaff is from Brainford (now Brentwood in Essex), and she is well known in Windsor. While the plot moves between the Garter Inn, Mistress Ford's house, the fields and Herne's oak in the Park, there is awareness of the close proximity of Windsor Castle and of the 'big city' of London from where some of the characters have come. The events in the forest may be just as fictive as those in the Forest of Arden or the Forest outside Athens, but the name itself would have had a real reference point for a contemporary audience as a semi-provincial, largely agricultural but regally significant town. All these details may simply be the consequence of the play having been commissioned and adapted to be played in Windsor, but since the play does not have to be played there (and usually is not), we can make the point that topical detail builds up a little world with its own rough town-plan, sports, occupations, friendships and rivalries, a rooted locality in which characters 'live', some permanently and some temporarily.

Much the same can be said, incidentally, of the settings of most of Shakespeare's comedies, even the most fantastical, for they are all essentially about people interacting in social groups. For example, through the accumulation of apparent and conspicuous irrelevancies of detail, Illyria, in *Twelfth Night*, is given a strong presence as a social setting which contains and is distinct from its citizens. The same could be said of Messina in *Much Ado About Nothing*, or the contrasted cities of Belmont and Venice in *The Merchant of Venice*. This is not just to make a point about atmosphere or background. The 'characterisation' of the town of Windsor extends to an underlying value-system, a set of tacit assumptions about the way life is, and should be, led. These attitudes may be espoused and practised by its citizens, but there is a feeling that they have been inherited from generations of Windsor-dwellers. They have the status of customary, unquestioned, and settled routines and beliefs. It is the solidity of these values which are tested and threatened by those who enter from the outside, in the clash which motivates the plot.

CIVILITY AND INCIVILITY

A brief exchange between Slender and Parson Evans reveals something of the underlying attitudes that bind Windsor society together. Slender regrets having become drunk in the company of Falstaff's men, since he has had his pocket picked as a consequence:

> Slender. . . . I'll ne'er be drunk whilst I live again, but in honest, civil, godly company, for this trick. If I be drunk, I'll be drunk with those that have the fear of God, and not with drunken knaves.
>
> Evans. So Got 'udge me, that is a virtuous mind.
>
> (i. i. 166–71)

Drunkenness is no vice in itself, but takes its colour from the company, as the local vicar confirms. In 'honest, civil, godly company' drunkenness may be the activity of a 'virtuous mind'. Honesty is almost next to godliness, separated only by 'civility'. The three qualities make one a good citizen, and it is this word that best sums up the ethos of Windsor. Mistress Quickly pays the highest compliment to Mistress Page:

> . . . and, let me tell you in your ear, she's as fartuous a civil modest wife, and one, I tell you, that will not miss your morning nor evening prayer, as any is in Windsor, who'er be the other.
>
> (ii. ii. 93–6)

Windsorites do not seem to have an exact definition of

civility, and they apply the concept mainly to keeping good company and attending church regularly. Basically, it is the kind of conduct that keeps the cogs of this society turning harmoniously. Making money may certainly be done 'in the way of honesty' as Mistress Quickly says (II. ii. 70–1), so long as any potential dishonesty is not visible. She herself is receiving money from two suitors to Anne Page, and she claims to be working for both of them, but she does it with 'discretion' (another Windsor word, used by Evans five times). Similarly, the Host of the Garter Inn makes money out of his tenants, and although he shows signs of deviousness and even roguish hypocrisy, he is trusted by all as honest and civil. The families that make up Windsor life (Pages, Fords and Shallows in particular) all show signs of being moderately prosperous, landowning and involved in trade or agriculture. Having money is, if anything, a sign of solid virtue. To historicise this aspect of the play, we could interpret the linkage between money-making, relative honesty, churchgoing and civility with the rise at the end of the sixteenth century of protestantism which eventually led to the clash between court and upper bourgeoisie that lay behind the English Revolution in the 1640s. Of course, such tensions are comically contained in this play, but they are latent as part of its 'world'.

Incivility is that which disrupts town life and significantly it is equated with ungodliness. 'There is no fear of Got in a riot' (I. i. 34) warns Parson Evans, commenting upon the nuisances committed by Falstaff and his men in their open 'coney-catching' (theft by deception), beating Shallow's men, killing his deer, and breaking open his lodge. Falstaff's men, in one sense or another, are identified with the London court and the aristocracy (as is Fenton) but ironically the real sin is their impecunity, their inability to pay their way. Non-payment of the rent at the Inn is as bad as the more open crimes. Whether Falstaff is down from London for a holiday or for the express purpose of making money, he is forced into deception by the very necessities of having to pay not only his own way but also those of his men, Pistol,

Bardolph and Nym and his page Robin. First he lays off Bardolph from his retinue by allowing him to work for the Host as a tapster (barman). Then he gets rid of Nym and Pistol in order to save money and to disassociate himself from their manifest crimes, thus entering into a state of 'French thrift' (I. iii. 79) by retaining only his 'skirted page', the boy Robin. His plans backfire since they give his former cronies the motive for betrayal and revenge.

It is 'thrift' (I. iii. 39), the need to pay one's way and to avoid at all costs 'waste' (ibid.) in money-conscious Windsor, that next prompts Falstaff to woo the wives, in a desperate attempt to gain access to their husbands' wealth. Mistress Page is, in his eyes, 'a region in Guiana, all gold and bounty' (I. iii. 64). He calls both 'exchequers' to him (ibid.) and sends his letters off to 'golden shores' (I. iii. 75). The imagery gives away his acquisitive motive. We shall see more evidence of commercial motivation in other characters, but the general point is that every single male character is driven by the need to make or maintain wealth. It is the central fact of (male) Windsor life, and the one that can either cause greatest havoc in society and in marriage, or conversely can keep everything in orderly, civil harmony.

Another quality which arouses the suspicions of people living in Windsor is, again in Parson Evans' word, 'affectations' (I. i. 140). He uses the word in reproof of Pistol's language, which is indeed grandiose, mannered ('He hears with ears' (I. i. 138)) and hyperbolical. Page, aroused to contempt by Falstaff's letter to his wife, says that he is 'a fellow frights English out of his wits', 'a drawling, *affecting* rogue' (II. i. 129–32, my italics). Suspicion of 'affectation' hangs over everybody who is in some way different or new: Fenton's courtly suavity (he speaks in iambic pentameters while Windsorites for the most part speak sober prose), Doctor Caius' Gallic English, as well as Falstaff's raffish and ostentatious crew are examples. Again, there is some irony in this, since some Windsorites speak in very individual ways and there are few examples of 'the King's English'. Parson Evans unconsciously draws humour from the audience, and from Falstaff who openly ridicules him, for his Welsh accent. Mistress Quickly commits malaprop-isms and amusing mishearings, the Host speaks with a bluff heartiness that does not carry the ring of sincerity, Shallow is easily sidetracked into irrelevancies and the speech of Simple and Slender is defined by their names. They are, in short, all to some extent at least linguistically eccentric and each could be described as 'affected'. The difference lies between acceptance and non-acceptance into Windsor. The ethos is fundamentally one that runs on conservativeness and conformity, where the familiar and habitual are con-sidered safe, while the new is intrusively dangerous. So long as the basic rules of civility (godliness, paying one's way, modesty, discretion and thrift) are observed, then all other divergences from a norm of behaviour will be tolerated and even overlooked. Mistress Page, for example, is sympathetic to Caius as a potential 'naturalised' Windsorite because he has money. But if these rules are not obeyed, or if outsiders are suspected on these grounds (as is Fenton), then all deviation of conduct will be regarded as 'affectation' and, generally speaking, as foreign to Windsor.

CLASS

Windsor is conservative also in its insistence on a stable hierarchy based on status and rank. So much is revealed in the exchange that opens the play:

> [Enter Justice Shallow, Slender, and Sir Hugh Evans]
> *Shallow.*   Sir Hugh, persuade me not. I will make a Star-Chamber matter of it. If he were twen-ty Sir John Falstaffs, he shall not abuse Robert Shallow, Esquire.
> *Slender.*   In the county of Gloucester, justice of peace and Coram.

Shallow.	Ay, cousin Slender, and Custalorum.
Slender.	Ay, and Ratolorum too. And a gentleman born, master parson, who writes himself Armigero – in any bill, warrant, quittance, or obligation, Armigero.
Shallow.	Ay, that I do, and have done any time these three hundred years.
Slender.	All his successors gone before him hath done't; and all his ancestors that come after him may. They may give the dozen white luces in their coat.
Shallow.	It is an old coat.

(I. i. 1–18)

What rankles with Shallow is that Falstaff is theoretically above him on the social scale, for Sir John is a knight while Shallow is an 'Esquire' and merely a provincial Justice of the Peace, however time-honoured the position. This inescapable fact is unaffected by the differences in wealth. Falstaff mercilessly uses his rank to defy the jurisdiction of Shallow's over him. The digression about Shallow's 'old coat' is fuelled by his impotent rage that although 'a gentleman born' and one that stands in a hereditary line, he can be upstaged and flouted by a penniless knight slumming from London.

Below Shallow in social standing are Ford and Page. They are landowners, moneyed citizens who are clearly accustomed to getting their own way in Windsor by working closely with Justice Shallow and dining with him frequently. They respect his authority as he respects their wealth and it is they (or more specifically Page) who set the standards of behaviour in the town. Page warns his daughter about the dangers of being wooed by Fenton because he is a courtly gentleman (although, like Falstaff, he needs money), nobly born and above her status. Page's class-suspiciousness is useful for the plot since he is motivated to act like the comic *senex*, the patriarchal figure who tries to prevent his daughter from marrying according to her desires. There may even be a parallel history to this situation, for if we may believe Mistress Quickly, Mistress Ford was unsuccessfully wooed by powdered gentlemen from court (II. iii. 60ff.) in an earlier siege of Windsor, before choosing the other local, landed yeoman, Ford. Page's choice for Anne's husband (and more pertinently the future recipient of his own money and status) is Shallow's nephew, Abraham Slender. Such a marriage would satisfy the men in Windsor, for it joins wealth and status, and keeps everything 'in the town'. Meanwhile, Mistress Page's choice is Doctor Caius, presumably because he is wealthy (he can pay his way at the Inn and can afford to pay Mistress Quickly and keep his man John Rugby), and also because a physician would have been respectably placed in status close to the parson-schoolmaster, Evans. Caius could also be expected to settle in Windsor, whereas Fenton would undoubtedly take Anne back to court. Both Mistress Page and her husband are able to overlook glaring personality defects in Doctor Caius and Slender respectively, because they place financial and class circumstances above the personal. In a sense Mrs Page is right in one thing at least. She wishes Anne to marry somebody who is in love with her and has no ulterior, fortune-hunting motive, and Caius seems to be sincere in his courtship. Equally, Anne is right in a deeper sense because, as well as not loving Caius, she also avoids the fate of Mistress Ford since the Doctor reveals himself to be as violently jealous as Ford.

Hugh Evans is deftly but unforgettably sketched as the local parson and schoolteacher. So convincing is he as a provincial schoolmaster that biographers scurry to the records to find a Welshman who may have taught Shakespeare in Stratford. His Welsh English is treated with contemptuous amusement by the aloofly metropolitan Falstaff, but he has clearly been fully accepted by Windsor for his professional contributions. Paradoxically for somebody who must once have been an 'outsider', Evans has established himself as a very central figure to the town's ethos, and it is he who expresses most overtly the high priority placed upon the god-fearing virtues and upon the sanctity of 'thrift'.

Some other characters, while definitely lower on the social scale than these, are socially indeterminate. The Host of the Garter Inn and Mistress Quickly need to make money where they can, and the economic imperative leads them to disguise or suppress their own opinions. They are go-betweens, useful to the dramatist for their accessibility to all classes high and low, which makes them ideal 'plotters'. While seeming trustworthy and even sycophantic to their social superiors, they prove themselves to the audience to be devious and hypocritical. The only judgements they make concern who can pay most. This mercenary quality may superficially appear to be a moral weakness, but before we condemn them we should acknowledge that their stations in life, respectively landlord of an ailing tavern with impecunious tenants and housekeeper to an erratic foreigner with a violent temper, are the least secure of any characters in the play. They must shift as they can to maintain a precarious living. Morals, in a town like Windsor, may be a luxury available only to those privileged with wealth. In a sense the modern equivalents of the Host and Mistress Quickly are the army of people in Britain today who depend on tourists, and who have an ambivalent attitude towards their employers, poised between obsequious flattery and disguised contempt.

Caius.	Rugby, come to the court with me. [To Mistress Quickly] By gar, if I have not Anne Page, I shall turn your head out of my door. Follow my heels, Rugby.
	[Exeunt Caius and Rugby]
Mistress Quickly.	You shall have – An fool's-head of your own. No, I know Anne's mind for that. Never a woman in Windsor knows more of Anne's

mind than I do, nor can do more
than I do with her, I thank heaven.
(I. iv. 120–6)

Beneath even these characters on the social scale are a bevy
of servants, more or less silent like John and Robert who are
Ford's servants and carry out the linen-basket containing
Falstaff, Jack Rugby who is Doctor Caius' servant, Robin,
Falstaff's page and Peter Simple, Slender's servant. In the
social hierarchy they are regarded more as embellishments
to their respective masters than as characters in their own
right. A condition of their service is that they keep quiet
about their employers' foibles and vices. If we look at the
dramatis personae with an eye to class, we discover that
characterisation is not so much a function of individualism
and inner identity (as is often assumed with Shakespearian
characters), but of economic station. Certainly, this is how
people in Windsor view and judge their neighbours.

INSIDERS AND OUTSIDERS

The structure of *The Merry Wives of Windsor* is built upon
the coherence of the society which we have just analysed.
The values held by Windsorites are tacitly agreed upon and
zealously defended. The society has a hierarchy, but there is
definitely a sense in which all those who are accepted share
the values of thrift, sobriety and social ranking. Justice
Shallow and Mr Page between them stand for what they see
as sensible qualities that bind them all together in a form of
trust. Oddities, eccentrics and even simpletons can be
accepted into the circle so long as they prove their tacit
agreement with an ethical and economic system. They are
the 'insiders'.

'Outsiders' are regarded with mistrust. Fenton is eventually accepted into the society, as, in a more provisional
way, is Doctor Caius. Falstaff is the most dangerous of all,
because he threatens the stable structure of Windsor values.

He is eventually purged in ritualistic fashion, as some sort of germ that must be ejected for the sake of the health of the society. And yet, as germs can be most threatening because their genetic make-up mirrors something in the organism they attack, so Falstaff (and in their different ways the more penitent and corrigible Fenton and Caius) simply clarifies, parodies and exaggerates tendencies already existent in Windsor. Ford is just as culpable as Falstaff in equating love with possession. His jealousy is simply the other side of Falstaff's desire to possess women in both sexual and commercial senses. It is Ford who pays Falstaff to test his wife's fidelity, saying 'if money go before, all ways do lie open' (II, ii. 164), words that are echoed by Falstaff in his own military idiom with 'Money is a good soldier, sir, and will on' (II. ii. 165). The Host of the Garter and Mistress Quickly are just as hypocritical and crafty as Falstaff in their readiness to take money for dubious causes. Anne Page and the 'merry wives' are just as devious in their plotting, though they can be seen as more effectively artful and also as more morally justifiable. Even Shallow, Page, Evans and Slender are as commercially-minded and acquisitive as Falstaff, although they, of course, would see their attitudes as prudent. The real danger of Falstaff is that he represents traits that already lie within the society of Windsor and must be kept under close control. His worst crime is to display in a kind of distorting mirror what all are like beneath the carefully maintained façade. This, more than his 'outsider' status, leads to his firm ejection from the society, and his final accommodation only at the cost of penitence and humiliation.

Christian values, modest but secure wealth, middling social status, prudent behaviour – these are the qualities which gain social acceptance and even respectability in Windsor. Difference of any kind is regarded as 'affectation' until the person is accepted by the community. The agreed values are defined as 'civil' and 'civic'. Gambling is not acceptable, and in a real sense both Falstaff and Fenton are gambling for women and wealth. High status is suspect, for why, the logic runs, would courtiers be in Windsor except to make money out of the town? 'Riotous' behaviour is frowned on and any form of excess, even excess in pleasure, is considered disruptive. Falstaff is excessive in body as in behaviour and he arouses most vilification. In such a society change will be resisted, the status quo preserved against all threats. Outsiders of any ilk are considered a risk to the stability of tradition and to the secure, generational rhythms of provincial English town life.

HISTORICAL CONTEXT

The historically-minded reader will want to draw a different set of conclusions from this analysis of Windsor. Just as the town is seen as a backwater under siege from the London court and Europe, so also can it be seen, in Elizabethan terms, as a bulwark of 'traditional' values which were being threatened in the late sixteenth century by the increasing dominance of London, and even by the threat posed by Queen Elizabeth marrying a foreigner in a diplomatically arranged marriage. Windsor is a town representative of a nostalgic concept of the 'organic community' based largely on agriculture and ancient status claimed now by a local, family-based hierarchy. It had its glorious past, as Mistress Quickly says, 'when the court lay at Windsor' (II. ii. 60–1), but its significance fell dramatically when the court was transferred to London and Windsor Palace had become something of a holiday-home for the monarchy rather than a political force. (As I have said, the play makes nothing of the Royal Palace except for this one, almost elegiac phrase.) It is a place which time has left behind but, in terms of the play, it is considered by the outside world as a catchment area for finance. Shallow, in his first appearance in *2 Henry IV*, is seen as inveterately nostalgic for his lost youth, his wild times at the Inns of Court where he studied Law with Falstaff. 'We have heard the chimes at midnight, Justice Shallow' (*2 Henry IV*, III. ii. 228) is Falstaff's weary contribution to the backward-looking mellowness of dimming memory. Even in *The Merry Wives* (where Falstaff has very clearly outstayed his welcome), Shallow itches to be young again to teach troublemakers a lesson with the sword. At the same time, Falstaff and Fenton are buccaneers, entrepreneurial risk-takers with their assets (Falstaff's rhetoric, Fenton's good looks and status) come to rob the town of its wealth. They are, at least in this respect, prototypes of the new capitalists, men in the sixteenth century forced by inflation into economic insecurity and destined to search for new worlds, to pirate foreign ships (Falstaff's imagery in this respect is telling), or marry into rural families in order to acquire a stronger economic basis. What is happening in Windsor provides a microcosm of what was happening in England in the 1590s in social and economic terms. The play gives a reflection of a tension between 'old', 'civil' and even feudal virtues and 'new', more dangerous but potentially profitable tendencies, the tension between an 'investment' and a 'risk-taking' mentality.

Shakespeare's insights into such social tensions are acute throughout his works, and in this he must have been helped by his own, socially mobile experience. He grew up in Stratford-upon-Avon, which cannot have been totally un-like Windsor as depicted in the play. He went to London to 'make his fortune' as an actor and playwright, and was so successful that he could play before the Queen in the acting company commissioned as The Queen's Men and, if legend is correct, he could even be commissioned to write a play at the request of Elizabeth. He was later to retire to Stratford to buy land and become one of the town's wealthiest men. If there is a 'moral' to the tale in the play, it may strike us as a provisional and perhaps suspect one. The older virtues of Windsor are glowingly presented at the end of the play as generous and forgiving ones, for both Fenton and even Falstaff are invited to the feast. If the older community on a cusp with threatening pressures may absorb the voguish – allow a little of the new into the settled verities of the old – it may survive unscathed and need not make major changes.

The sardonic mind may see this as a moral which is deeply comforting to those who inherit the wealth of England, deeply unjust and pessimistic to those who do not have a place in the ordered hierarchy created by wealth. It was a complacency to be challenged in succeeding centuries but which might still have its legacy in England today.

· 2 ·

Women

Just as there is a confrontation between insiders and outsiders in Windsor, so there is a more underground battle waged between women and men. As the men try to organise even affairs of the heart in a commercially-minded way, so the women work hard to subvert such practices. Various revenges are carried out in the play, as the critic Linda Anderson has stressed, and at the most general level these may be interpreted as revenges of women against men. Just as disruptive outsiders must first be punished and then accommodated, so must men be punished by women before reconciliation may occur. The obvious vehicle for this strand of the play is the narrative concerning Falstaff's wooing of the 'merry wives' and Ford's jealousy, but it is equally observable in the parallel plot concerning the wooing of Anne Page.

The range of attitudes held by men of Windsor towards the women can be surveyed by following through the story of the young Anne Page. Her name is introduced very early in connection with potential marriage, and the whole dialogue is worth examining:

Evans.   And there is also another device in my prain, which peradventure prings goot discretions

Slender.

Evans.

Shallow.

Evans.

Shallow.

Evans.

with it. There is Anne Page, which is daughter to Master George Page, which is pretty virginity.

Mistress Anne Page? She has brown hair, and speaks small like a woman?

It is that fery person for all the 'orld, as just as you will desire. And seven hundred pounds of moneys, and gold, and silver, is her grandsire upon his death's-bed – Got deliver to a joyful resurrections! – give, when she is able to overtake seventeen years old. It were a goot motion if we leave our pribbles and prabbles, and desire a marriage between Master Abraham and Mistress Anne Page.

Did her grandsire leave her seven hundred pound?

Ay, and her father is make her a petter penny.

I know the young gentlewoman. She has good gifts.

Seven hundred pounds, and possibilities, is goot gifts.

(I. i. 40–60)

Anne is described in terms of a series of physical characteristics. 'Pretty virginity' stresses her sexual status and implies her readiness for marriage, while 'brown hair, and speaks small like a woman' emphasises the difference between man and woman. Shallow's reference to her 'good gifts' is not amplified by him, so whether he means personal skills and qualities we shall never know. Anne's most striking quality to the men is her dowry. Seven hundred pounds from her grandfather when she reaches seventeen, and more from her father, is to them her greatest attraction. The subject is gleefully introduced by Parson Evans, followed up with interest by Shallow and clinched triumphantly in Evans' 'Seven hundred pounds, and possibilities, is goot gifts'. A marriage between Abraham Slender and Anne Page is more or less arranged on this basis. The idea may never have entered Slender's mind, but now that it is raised he becomes nervous at her entrance ('O heaven! This is Mistress Anne Page' (I. i. 176)) and thereafter 'Sweet Anne Page' is his refrain. He yearns for his Book of Songs and Sonnets, presumably to read love poems. The subject of marriage is not put to Anne, but to Slender, who, whether coyly or imperiously, agrees to marry her 'upon any reasonable demands' (I. i. 210). He is not able to say whether he can love her or not, but he will, upon the request from his uncle and 'upon good dowry' (I. i. 222) which is Evans' obsession, at least marry her. There are signs of developing embarrassment, if not love, in Slender's behaviour, for he loses his appetite on her reappearance, and he finds it difficult to converse with her except in terms of male preoccupations such as violent sports which 'women, indeed, cannot abide' (I. i. 278). He manages to boast that he has a 'man' (Simple), that he keeps 'but three men and a boy' until his mother dies, and lives 'like a poor gentleman born', all presumably designed to impress her by his class aspirations. Anne appears oblivious to his confusion, and reiterates that she was simply sent to call him for dinner.

The exchanges may simply take their place in the long history in English romantic comedy of courtship, but they also etch in certain attitudes which underlie all the males' attitudes during the play. The elders speak of the woman as little more than a dowry, an investment for the highest bidder, with lip-service only paid to concepts of love. They certainly do not consult any woman in an affair which looks increasingly like a business transaction. Moreover, it is demonstrated that the man in question, Slender, is completely unable or unwilling to communicate with Anne except in male terms and by defining the woman as 'other', as one who does not like bear-baiting.

These attitudes towards Anne persist. We learn very soon that the foreigner Doctor Caius is in love with her, and he becomes violently jealous when he learns of Slender's competition, threatening to kill Evans for his support of Slender's cause:

> By gar, I vill kill de Jack priest. And I have appointed mine host of de Jarteer to measure our weapon. By gar, I will myself have Anne Page.
>
> (I. iv. 113–16)

It is not the only time in the play when male jealousy breaks into murderous rage. When men are not seeing Anne as a possession to be bought and sold, they are seeing her as a prize to be won, by violent means if necessary. Luckily in this case the plotting and active diplomacy of the Host of the Garter helps to avoid bloodshed, since he sends the participants in the duel to different places. The role of Mistress Quickly is highly dubious, because she is quite happy to act as go-between for any number of Anne's suitors who can pay. Her loyalty to a fellow woman is tempered by her own financial needs. After assuring Caius that Anne loves him, she immediately swears to Fenton that he is preferred. However, Mistress Quickly, at the cost of any consistency to her character, facilitates the final revenge upon the men of Windsor by orchestrating the end of the play. By choosing her to play the Queen of the Fairies, Shakespeare perhaps implies that it is her protean qualities that suit the pivotal figure in this scene of disguises and tricks.

We know from experience of theatrical love conventions that Fenton will be the one who ends up marrying Anne, for he is high-born, neither foreign nor imbecilic, he speaks poetry rather than the prevailing prose, and Anne loves him. We discover her preference at the beginning of III. iv, and here also her father's implacable resistance to Fenton's suit is made clear. There is considerable irony in the objection that Page has to Fenton. He says that the down-on-his-luck courtier is simply after Anne's money and that he can love her 'but as a property' (III. iv. 10). Page himself, of course, regards Anne in much the same light, even if his preference is for a different man. Anne notes the irony when Slender enters:

> . . . This is my father's choice.
> O, what a world of vile ill-favoured faults
> Looks handsome in three hundred pounds a year!
>
> (III. iv. 31–3)

It is clear that Page himself is marrying off his daughter 'but as a property' to the bidder of his choice, for economic and family reasons. Page's own language betrays his motives when he angrily tells Fenton his daughter is 'disposed of' (III. iv. 68) when he refers to Slender as his 'son'. In his mind, his daughter's intentions or feelings are irrelevant to her 'choice' in marriage.

Shakespeare could easily have made Fenton entirely pure and innocent in his motives, but significantly in this dramatist's ironic gaze, Fenton is not entirely free of the male materialism. Although reformed by apparently genuine love for Anne, he is not above reproach initially. He speaks himself of 'My riots past, my wild societies' (he is said to have been with 'the wild Prince [Hal] and Poins' and therefore has some association with Falstaff and his men (III. ii. 67)), and he even ingenuously admits that his motives were at first mercenary:

> Albeit, I will confess, thy father's wealth
> Was the first motive that I wooed thee, Anne;
> Yet, wooing thee, I found thee of more value
> Than stamps in gold or sums in seal'd bags.
> And 'tis the very riches of thyself
> That now I aim at.
>
> (III. iv. 12–17)

This declaration is enough to satisfy the conventions of the romantic suitor, but perhaps not quite enough to suppress the disquieting realisation that Slender has also anticipated that love might follow a mercenary marriage. Fenton's imagery of 'value' still couches his thoughts in terms of gold and money. The hints about Fenton's underlying commercialism are, strictly speaking, unnecessary, and their inclusion reinforces the reading that all men, at heart, regard women as property. Romantic comedy does not encourage us to speculate too closely upon future relations in marriage, and Anne is able, with the help of the Host, to avoid the fate of marrying either Slender or Caius, and instead marries the man of her own choice and for love. Fenton rather self-righteously is at the end able to turn the accusation against Anne's 'disobedience, or unduteous title' (v. v. 219) into a defence of marriage for love and an attack on forced marriage (222) – rather than into a defence of Anne's independent right to choose her husband. Although Shakespeare is, in Elizabethan terms, being liberal in his attitude to marriage for love, there is still a subtle division in the presentation of Fenton who is willing to agree that Anne has committed both 'offence' and 'deceit' or 'craft' (218–9) against her parents which can be justified only in the name of love. He does not admit complicity with offence, deceit and craft himself. And so in his eyes the woman, while made the passive or acquiescent object of the male pursuit without a mind of her own, is simultaneously the one who is actively treacherous. He cannot really have it both ways, but he is by no means the only man in this play who claims just this. Ford is equally culpable, not just when he is jealous but right to the very end when he claims to give a 'moral' to the action and inadvertently reveals the persisting assumption that women are objects to be 'sold' while also agents to be blamed for 'offence':

> In love the heavens themselves do guide the state.
> Money buys lands, and wives are *sold* by fate.
>
> (v. v. 224–5, my italics)

Coming from Ford such a statement can be seen as the re-assertion of his own sense of self-importance as the 'buyer' in a marriage where he had believed his position as 'owner' to be undermined by his wife's choices – an acknowledgement and rationalisation of the uncontrollability of female sexuality which throughout has haunted him, although he can now afford complacently to ignore it.

Before leaving Anne Page, we should turn our attention

from the limitations of her situation as it is controlled by
male attitudes (including Fenton's) and focus on her own
actions. Throughout, she has shown herself willing to resist
pressures, actively, forcibly and even courageously. She
flatly rejects the 'vile ill-favoured faults' (III. iv. 32) of
Slender, tests Fenton's sincerity by challenging him to deny
her father's suspicions (III. iv. 11) and ridicules the idea of
marrying Caius with a vehemence and vivacity that indicate
not only her spiritedness but her ingenuity in metaphor:

> Alas, I had rather be set quick i'th'earth,
> And bowled to death with turnips.
>
> (III. iv. 84–5)

She is finally successful in marrying according to her desires,
by taking practical measures to include the Host in the plot
of her own devising. However, it must be emphasised that
no matter how assertive are her actions, no matter how
complete is her triumph, they are enacted in resistance to
coercion and to manipulation carried out in a male context.
Rather cynically, it is Fenton's bribing of the Host with a
hundred pounds in gold (IV. vi. esp. 5) that is needed before
the plot is finally put into action.

The part of the narrative concerning Falstaff's pursuit of
Mistresses Page and Ford is initially fuelled by the combina-
tion of Falstaff's pecuniary problems and by his monumental
vanity:

> O, she did so course o'er my exteriors with such a greedy
> intention that the appetite of her eye did seem to scorch
> me up like a burning-glass. Here's another letter to her.
> She bears the purse too. She is a region in Guiana, all gold
> and bounty. I will be cheaters to them both, and they shall
> be exchequers to me. They shall be my East and West
> Indies, and I will trade to them both. . . .
>
> (I. iii. 60–7)

The imagery immediately marks out Falstaff as, literally,
a fortune-hunter. References to trade with the East and
West Indies would have been topical in the 1590s, a period

of imperialistic endeavour by profit-seeking entrepreneurs. The passage also shows that Falstaff bases his conception of love on the sexual desires of women, their 'appetite'. He says nothing of his own feelings, amatory or otherwise, while complacently assuming that the two married women of Windsor are burning with lust for his fat body. Just as the men hold responsible Anne Page as the volatile cause of love in others while at the same time denying her any active part in courtship, so is Falstaff holding responsible the women for making overtures to him while he plans to conduct the affair on his own terms. These terms are entirely dictated by his need to extract money from some source or other.

He miscalculates in at least three ways. First, he does not realise that by dismissing Pistol and Nym from his service in order to save money, he gives them the perfect excuse for revenge. They immediately inform Page and Ford of Falstaff's designs on their wives. Secondly, he cannot know the consequences of Mr Ford's jealousy. In Ford's possessiveness we have a Windsorite equivalent to Falstaff's acquisitiveness. Their attitude to the women as little more than commodities to be bought and sold by sex is almost indistinguishable. We have already been told by Mistress Ford that her husband is congenitally jealous, and we immediately see his suspicions awakened – not of Falstaff but of his wife – when Nym reveals the plot. While Page dismisses the possibility of his wife accepting the advances of Falstaff, and contemptuously scorns the 'drawling, affecting rogue' (II. i. 132), Ford mutters aside 'I will be patient. I will find out this' (II. i. 119). While Page instantly sees through the motives of Nym and Pistol as 'very rogues, now they be out of service' (II. i. 163–4), Ford finds them 'good sensible fellow[s]' (II. i. 135) and is inclined to trust them before his wife. Othello's willingness to trust 'honest' Iago before Desdemona turns on a similar division between men and women. Ford claims not to 'misdoubt' his wife (II. i. 173) and yet he scorns Page as 'a secure fool' who 'stands so firmly on his wife's frailty' (II. i. 215–16) and determines to find out the truth for himself. It is clear that he sees the

enemy not as Falstaff but as his wife's 'frailty'. His
assumption is exactly Falstaff's – women's sexuality is a
commodity that can be bought with flattery and, in Falstaff's estimation, can be turned into money. Money becomes a familiar nexus between men as Ford, disguised as
Brook, strikes a bargain with Falstaff to test his wife:

Ford.	. . . if money go before, all ways do lie open.
Falstaff.	Money is a good soldier, sir, and will on.
Ford.	Troth, and I have a bag of money here troubles me . . .

(II. ii. 164–6)

Ford in his jealousy is no better than Falstaff in his sexual
profiteering, and although one is an insider and the other an
outsider, they are inextricably linked. Revenge over Falstaff
must also be revenge over something within the Windsor
male enclave, personified in Ford's behaviour.

The revenge, of course, belongs to the women, and
Falstaff's third miscalculation lies in not foreseeing that the
women, less competitive and more collaborative than the
men, will confer with each other and interpret the situation
as one in which women are pitted against men. In fact, far
from being flattered by an impecunious knight's advances,
they are furious at his arrogance. In itself, this fact may
reflect the new status and self-esteem of middle-class
women in Elizabethan England, showing them unable to
feel any kind of deference towards a person higher on the
social scale who is not virtuous, respectable or even sober.
Falstaff seems to assume his title is enough to dazzle the
wives of Windsor. As soon as Mistress Ford receives the
letter from Falstaff she hastens to Mistress Page who is
fulminating over the identical letter she has received. The
latter is already seeing the battle as one between women and
men, and she is vowing revenge:

Mistress Page.	. . . Why, I'll exhibit a bill in the parliament for the putting down of men. How shall I be revenged on

Mistress Page.   him? For revenged I will be, as sure as his guts are made of puddings.

                   (II. i. 26–9)

In their 'counsel' together (II. i. 39) the women discover that Falstaff's letters are worded exactly alike except for the names, prompting Mistress Page to exclaim 'I warrant he hath a thousand of these letters, writ with blank space for different names – sure, more – and these are of the second edition' (II. i. 69–71). Mistress Ford is just as bent on revenge, and there is more than a hint that she is contemplating revenge on her jealous husband at the same time: '. . . O that my husband saw this letter! It would give eternal food to his jealousy' (II. i. 93–4).

At this point in the plot, we might note a little contrapuntal touch which clinches that aspect of the dramatic design highlighting the underlying conflict between men's aggressiveness and women's co-operation. Falstaff's letter, while chivalrous in its tone, presents itself as one expressing 'the love of a soldier', eschewing the term 'pity me' because '' 'tis not a soldier-like phrase' (II. i. 10–11). The next shift of the narrative is to the other plot, as the men enter full of the impending duel between Evans and Caius over the hand of Anne Page. The Host's repeated greetings of 'cavaliero' and 'knight' again draw the military allusion as they speak of measuring the weapons, and even the 'man of peace' Justice Shallow finds his finger itching when he sees a sword out (II. iii. 41–2). The duellists, ironically enough, will be a doctor and a parson, the latter vowing to 'knog his urinals about his knave's costard' (III. i. 13–14). Whichever way we look, there is a common link between the men of fighting over women. Fortunately, they are all cowards. The one go-between in this general distancing of the interests of men and women is Mistress Quickly; just as she is willing to aid any of Anne's suitors who is able to pay her, so she allays Falstaff's momentary doubt that Mistresses Ford and Page have conferred with each other, and she at least pretends to help him (II. ii. 100ff.) (although presumably at this point she is in league with the wives). Pistol sees Mistress Quickly as his own target, and again his image of taking a 'prize' is one from the language of piracy:

> This punk is one of Cupid's carriers.
> Clap on more sails; pursue; up with your fights;
> Give fire! She is my prize, or ocean whelm them all.
>
> (II. ii. 131–4)

The long scene ends with Ford in soliloquy ranting and railing in his jealousy over the term 'cuckold' and over the untrustworthiness of women: 'Would any man have thought this? See the hell of having a false woman!' (II. ii. 276–7). His real fear is that his reputation amongst the men of Windsor has been 'gnawn at' (II. ii. 279). The battle-lines are drawn up between the sexes, and the rest of the play shows the women to be superior in wit and strategy.

The interrelated revenge plots carried out by the women over both Falstaff and Ford provide the high comedy of the whole play. Of course, dramatic creations are not real-life people, and the true guile belongs to the playwright in his skilful control, but it is significant that his mastery over the plot is carried in the 'plotting' in the conspiratorial sense by the women. Not just once but three times Mistresses Ford and Page lure Falstaff into the boudoir with hopes of love and money. On the first two occasions Ford is also ambushed into humiliating retreat in front of the menfolk of Windsor, as Falstaff first escapes hidden in a dirty-linen basket (to be dumped unceremoniously in the Thames), and then escapes disguised as the old woman of Brainford under the nose of the unsuspecting Ford. The second scene is almost an emblem of the confusion over gender created by the men, as the fat knight, disguised as a woman, is beaten by the jealous husband who happens to hate the old woman, along with, one feels, all women. In both scenes (III. iii and IV. ii) Mistress Ford is unashamed in her double pleasure: 'I know not which pleases me better – that my husband is deceived, or Sir John' (III. iii. 166–7). The darker side of the situation is revealed by Mistress Quickly when she reports that after the second incident 'Mistress Ford, good heart, is beaten black and blue, that you cannot see a white spot about her' (IV. v. 102–4), and although Quickly does not always tell the truth, we have no reason to doubt her reminder of the blatant violence of Ford's character and of the physical danger stemming from the actions of men in the play.

The third revenge over Falstaff comes in the scene at Herne's oak at midnight, and although it is presented as the more comprehensive revenge of Windsor over the dangerous outsider, it can equally be seen as a ritualistic revenge of women over men and the culmination of this thread of the plot. Ford by now has apparently been converted to faith in his wife's loyalty, although the fact that we are not shown his transformation may signify that we should suspect it. He becomes the scourge of Falstaff, and all his violence is transferred hysterically from women to the knight in revenge for his own humiliation: 'Now sir, who's a cuckold now? Master Brook' (v. v. 109–11). (We do not now use the image of horns for cuckoldry, but for the Elizabethans the very sight of Falstaff wearing them would centralise in this scene the subject of male rivalry and jealousy.) When Evans reads a little sermon to Falstaff, Ford chimes in with 'Well said, fairy Hugh' only to be reprimanded himself:

> Evans.   And leave your jealousies too, I pray you.
> Ford.   I will never mistrust my wife again till thou art able to woo her in good English.
>
> (v. v. 131–3)

It may be a peculiarly modern response to say that Ford cannot even express penitence without a racial joke. As Ford's crescendo of abuse against Falstaff rises ('a hodge-pudding . . . bag of flax . . . slanderous as Satan . . .' (v. v. 150ff.)) we may even feel some sense of injustice, especially when the main accusation Ford levels against Falstaff is that of tricking him out of money – a not-so-subtle self-deception on Ford's part, since he was only too willing to give the money to test his wife's virtue. In drawing some of our pity, Falstaff makes us see that, in the terms of Northrop Frye, he is being made a scapegoat for sins that have been latent (and sometimes blatant) in Windsor itself. He has acted as a catalyst for the unleashing of forces already present in Windsor but normally in complacent fashion not directly faced. His own phrase implies the more general revenge which has come to a head in the scene: 'When night-dogs run, all sorts of deer are chased' (v. v. 230).

Both Ford and Falstaff may be seen as legitimate victims of what the English Renaissance viewed as a tradition of 'gossips'. This word, as Linda Woodbridge points out, could be used favourably or unfavourably. It could mean idle, tattling women, more or less as we use the word gossip today, or it could be used by women of their close female friends and confidantes. The second association is clearly the one relevant to the merry wives in the play. Whereas the men tend to be competitive, individualistic and collaborative only in what they view as financial matters such as marrying Anne Page to Slender, the women share knowledge and ideas and make their plots together. There was a tradition in the drama of men being somewhat apprehensive of women banding together, and indeed the practice no doubt emerged at least in part as a response to male interference in their lives and threats to their interests and social autonomy. Ford is deeply suspicious not just of his wife but of what he sees as a conspiratorial cabal between the wives which challenges his authority within marriage. In the event, his suspicions become the target of the comedy and satire, and little sympathy is spared for him.

The women's triumph is completed in the final scene by the evidence of all sorts of gender-inversions. Evans, dressed as a satyr, is aligned implicitly with the women and the fairies ('Heavens defend me from that Welsh fairy' blusters Falstaff at v. v. 81), and the suitors of Anne Page are tricked out of their 'prize' by Fenton and Anne herself. Slender has been married to 'a great lubberly boy . . . a postmaster's boy' (v. v. 181; 184–5) in woman's apparel. This is not only humiliating for Slender but for Page as well since he was supporting Slender. It is telling that he can say 'Did not I tell you how you should know my daughter by her garments?' (v. v. 190–1) since he has always regarded his daughter as an expensive object, a garment, rather than a person with feelings. He is forced now simply to accept her marriage to Fenton: 'Well, what remedy? . . . What cannot be eschewed must be embraced' (v. v. 228–9). Meanwhile, the other suitor, Doctor Caius, has also married '*un garçon*, a boy; *un paysan*, by gar, a boy' (v. v. 200–1). He too has judged only by appearances, taking the one 'in green' who happens to be male. The extra, 'metatheatrical' irony is that *all* the actors on the Elizabethan stage were males.

It would seem, then, that the women in the play have ample cause to rejoice in a comic victory over the darker side of men, their possessiveness, lust, jealousy and violence. And yet, at the end we might pause to question whether anything has really changed in the social order or in the ordering of gender relations. Mistress Page, exercising the conciliatory tone that has been a defining characteristic of the women in their dealings with each other, chooses not to emphasise a female interpretation of events, and instead she packs all the story away as simply a funny tale:

> Good husband, let us every one go home,
> And laugh this sport o'er by a country fire;
> Sir John and all.
>
> (v. v. 233–5)

Even Falstaff can be accommodated into the festivities, remade in his degradation as a humble, Windsor 'insider' (if only for one night) because others feel comfortable that the threat he poses has been brought into the open and exorcised. None draws attention to the more internal threat within this society, and it may even be a sardonic dramatist who returns the last words to the most dangerous man of all, ending with a bawdy quip that implies little more status to his wife than that of a bedfellow:

Ford.   Let it be so. Sir John,
            To Master Brook you yet shall hold your word,
            For he tonight shall lie with Mistress Ford.
                                          (v. v. 235–7)

The question raised in the Introduction of whether Shakespeare radically challenges or merely underwrites the politics of male supremacy governing Windsor can probably be answered in genuinely different ways according to one's point of view. Before we too readily condemn him, however, it is worth noting that his women characters are given far more autonomy of action and power than those of other dramatists of the time, and when they are 'put in their place' more potential audience regret is authorised by the action. In a play which is often compared with *The Merry Wives*, Dekker's *The Shoemaker's Holiday*, women are largely excluded from any active role and no voice speaks of their subjugation. Citizenship is here entirely a male concept. Rose is treated as a commodity by all characters and she has none of Anne Page's freedom at least to resist choices made for her. Whereas Anne is seen as a vital, young woman resisting an ageing, commercially-minded community (including even her mother) Rose is not seen as anything more than a docile property of her future husband, and the play itself does not build in another view. The plight of Jane, who marries a man who is conscripted for the wars and comes back without a leg, is seen as lamentable, but in this situation the real target of Dekker's raw-edged criticism is the system that deprives the man of freedom, rather than the woman. Meanwhile, the character who could be compared with Mistress Quickly, Margery Eyre, is treated as simply bumbling and amusing, and her husband boasts that he saved her 'from selling tripes in Eastcheap' (vii. 69–70). If a fully sympathetic, feminist reading of Shakespeare's comedies must rely on the extent to which an audience feels justified by the play to object to female entrapment, then at least there are voices within the play that allow such conclusions. This applies whether or not the women by the end are compelled simply to fall back into stereotyped roles (such as Ford's sexual partner) rather than women with minds of their own. In Dekker's play and most others of the time there is simply no possibility of mounting such an argument since the dramatist has clearly not anticipated the woman's position being taken so sympathetically.

In *The Merry Wives of Windsor* questions of gender construction and the role of women are bound up also with the more general issues of emotional relationships conducted in a social context. As in all Shakespeare's plays, convention is played off against an abrasive reality, in an ironic vision which can both value and devalue both attitudes. In the Anne–Fenton relationship, for example, the conventional pattern is inherited from aristocratic, courtly love. Fenton conducts it in poetry as if to raise the register from the more prosaic society he has entered. It springs from genuine love and a romantic attitude, and it has an illicit and clandestine element in having to be hidden from parents, as courtly love in its earliest form often involved adultery. However, there are big divergences from the literary norm. Fenton is the one who is high-born, Anne middle-class, whereas in courtly love the woman was traditionally socially superior. In the tradition the woman was disdainful and unresponsive, giving just enough encouragement for the man to persist in his attentions but not giving herself. Anne, on the contrary, is as keen on the relationship as Fenton. She does not conceal her love, and after testing the man's sincerity she takes equal responsibility in the pursuit of marriage. The plot involving Falstaff and the wives is almost the reverse. It would seem to have less to do with courtly love than with the mercenary aims associated with Citizen Comedy. All the characters are mature rather than innocently young. They are all open-eyed and without illusions about what is happening. However, this 'realistic' stratum is complicated by elements from the love code. Falstaff writes love-letters (an essential ingredient) and his rhetoric is chivalrous and martial. The 'affairs' are conducted secretly and on the understanding that they would be adulterous if pursued. In parody of the woman of courtly love, Mistress Page and Mistress Ford present themselves as by turns encouraging and rejecting. Disdain is at least on the spectrum towards the complete lack of interest the women have in Falstaff, and towards the private fury they feel about his conduct. In both sets of relationships, convention is fused with realism, and realism is overlaid with conventions.

The third kind of relationship depicted is equally double-edged for women but in a different kind of way. Marriage is the third estate in the play, and it is presented in radically opposing lights. The marriage between the Pages is serenely exemplary: Page totally trusts his wife and she protects his interests. In return, she seems to live in a state of freedom, as Mistress Quickly puts it:

> Never a wife in Windsor leads a better life than she does. Do what she will, say what she will, take all, pay all, go to bed when she list, rise when she list, all is as she will. And truly, she deserves it; for if there be a kind woman in Windsor, she is one.
>
> (II. ii. 113–18)

Even though she is in the act of tricking Falstaff, there seems no reason to doubt Quickly's evaluation of Mistress Page's marital situation. If we can suppress our reservations that Page is a complacent bore, we can see their marriage as based on firm companionship and trust, an example of the kind of relationship which Shakespeare himself made into a convention which stood against the volatile fire and ice of romantic, courtly love. On the contrary, marriage for Mistress Ford is little more than a trap. Her husband has a record of mistrust and suspicion of his wife, and he goes to the length of acting as spy on her. The only way she can escape the constrictions is to trick him and then humiliate him in revenge.

At the very least we must admit that Shakespeare is unusual in his own time in respectfully representing female consciousness as in the ascendance, and in allowing women, if only temporarily, an assertiveness of their own which controls the plot. In each situation in which the women find themselves, they are allowed to exercise initiative and they are never docile, even if it should also be added that they must simply react to men's initiatives rather than pursuing independent goals of their own. We cannot say whether Shakespeare is reflecting a social reality, although there is some evidence that English women under a female monarch were seen as having more freedom than women in Europe:

> What confirmes the liberty of our women more in *England*, then the Italian Proverbe, which saies if there were a bridge over the narrow Seas, all the women in *Italy* would shew their husbands a Million of light paire of heeles, and flie over into *England*?
>
> (Dekker and Webster, *Westward Ho*, iii. iii. 85–8, quoted Woodbridge p. 171)

Equally, it is impossible to say whether Shakespeare himself in writing the play was condoning or condemning the fact that the women do not have more freedom to dictate the terms of the action. The question of the justice or injustice of the final situation as we leave the play may not matter so much to our understanding of Shakespeare's play as to our heightened awareness of the world in which we live. If drama can alert us to the existence of injustice or limitation in our own society, then it has surely exerted some sort of educative function.

· 3 ·

Structures

Until quite recently some works of literature, and particularly Shakespeare's plays, used to be analysed as if they were spontaneous products of the imagination which had 'organic unity' emanating or growing from a 'deep centre' in the writer's imagination. Nowadays, there is a greater recognition (and here ironically we may be seeing a return to much older forms of criticism rather than a fundamental discovery of the late twentieth century) that plays are *made*, and that in the making the writer is building up a series of structures within structures. Modern structuralists have emphasised the element of construction from given patterns and forms, almost to the exclusion of content, while their successors, deconstructionists, have dismantled the constructions in an attempt to examine clearly and without obfuscation the underlying attitudes which generate works. No longer can words like 'universal', 'genius', 'originality' and 'unity' be used with any innocence of a work of literature, or art or popular culture for that matter. Statements by critics, equally, can never again be treated as being 'impartial', 'detached' or 'objective', since criticism too has been seen as a constructed artefact underpinned by ideology, unstated attitudes and definable if usually concealed social and political attitudes.

As was hinted in the parentheses above, Shakespeare would almost certainly have been surprised to think of these concepts as a great discovery made nearly four centuries after his plays were written. All Renaissance literary theory emphasises the fact that a work of literature is a construction using building blocks such as source plots, rules of rhetoric and conventions, rather than an upwelling of inspired, individual insight. Certainly there was a place for *inventio* in writers' attitudes, but more importantly they were trying to 'imitate' classical models rather than to be original. One proof of this comes in the fact that Shakespeare 'made up' very few of his stories, and often even the language is surprisingly close to that of his sources. In the case of *The Merry Wives*, imitation in the narrowest sense is not an issue since it is one of the three plays which has no single, identifiable model or source, but the larger questions remain. It is self-evident from the dramatist's profession and from the finished products that more care was taken over structuring the plays down to the level of detail than in trying to create consistent characters, or to work through clusters of imagery, or to be full of gnomic 'insight'. Furthermore, since Renaissance theorists placed drama and literature in the categories of 'rhetoric', the art of persuasion and learning, rather than in that of diverting entertainment, they clearly had some conception of trying to 'teach' and therefore to persuade us of the rightness of certain underlying, ideological positions, to use terms from modern criticism.

All this is not meant to deny the possibility of Shakespeare's plays giving us new insights into our own societies and lives, nor is it to denigrate the subtle and sophisticated minds that have recently dismantled some of the most cherished notions of nineteenth- and early twentieth-century critics. It is intended, rather, to 'demystify' (another word of recent coinage) the plays of Shakespeare and to justify us in looking soberly and without reverential awe at how these systems of structure are built up, and how they can affect an audience or reader. When we do so, we find that a play like *The Merry Wives of Windsor* is created with not just one structural principle operating from within (the assumption behind some notions of 'unity'), but instead with layers of structures from the most inclusive level of plot down to the minutiae of constructed language. Language is discussed later; in this chapter we shall look at the crafty plotting in the play, at the use of the scene as a fundamental structuring device, and then at some discontinuities which appear to cut across the illusion of seamlessness which calculated structuring can create.

PLOTTING

If nothing else, *The Merry Wives* is a play that is extremely skilful in its interweaving of diverse but interconnected stories. It is a very busy play, but the skill comes in the dramatist's clarity of presentation, which is so effective that many critics have regarded it as straightforward and simple. To pick up the weaving metaphor, the strong warps are two quite unrelated plots which guide our expectations towards separate conjectured conclusions, and the wefts are the packing and hatching of incidents and language to create the moment-by-moment texture, dramatic colour and local variety. Not much time need be spent on this aspect of Shakespeare's craftsmanship, since once it is pointed out it is obvious. The two plots cannot be separated into 'plot' and 'sub-plot' since neither can be seen as subsidiary to the other. Both are introduced almost immediately at the start of the play.

The more straightforward plot (so far as audience expectations are concerned) is the wooing of Anne Page. We quickly deduce that Anne will not marry Slender or Doctor Caius, but that she will marry Fenton. Even such simple certainty is given maximum complication by the fact that each wooer has cheering supporters, and these supporters believe they have some influence over Anne or some right to choose her marriage partner for her. Her father and the town's male population support Slender, while her mother and (at least for much of the time) Mistress Quickly support the case of Caius. Meanwhile, Anne makes up her own mind early on and the only 'suspense' lies in how the desired end will be brought about. The end is made, of course, by the dramatist, the master-plotter, in the scene in the forest when confusion of identity reigns, but the impression is that he has delegated the task to 'plotters' within the story, the Host of the Garter who, for money, helps Anne and Fenton towards marriage, the wives, and Mistress Quickly. When it is unravelled, this thread is seen to be far more adroitly handled and complex than at first appears. It could, indeed, have been quite enough to fuel one substantial play.

As if to make life harder for himself, Shakespeare added the equally insistent plot of Falstaff and the wives. In terms of audience expectations this is much more open-ended and freewheeling. All that Falstaff really needs or wants is money. In theory at least two conclusions are possible – the triumph of Falstaff in bedding the women and getting access to their purses; or the final revenge taken by the women on him for his arrogant presumptuousness and by the town for his callous attempts at exploitation. In fact the second fairly soon becomes the expected option, and again the fun comes not in the surprise of what will happen but in *how* it will happen, a process including the dunking of the fat knight in the Thames inside a dirty-linen basket, his disguise as a fat woman who is beaten, and his final humiliation before the whole township at Herne's oak. Once again, the skill in deploying these events into a single curve of narrative development must be admired when it is inspected in its own right.

Further admiration is required when we realise that not only is this plot resolved at the same time as the former one, but that it is itself overlaid with a related but separate one which was to motivate a whole play in *Othello* and half a play in *The Winter's Tale*. I mean the story of Ford's jealousy, which drives him into disguise and into extreme states of passion. Of course, this 'serious' plot is generated by the 'comic' Falstaff one, but in a sense it runs independently alongside in its own feverish sequence, which for Ford is painful and degrading, for Mistress Ford a legitimate revenge on her husband, and for the audience a source of comedy.

Timely reminder of the amusement generated by each plot demonstrates that comedy itself is a structure which is predominantly a function of plot, at least in Shakespeare. Critics who revere Shakespeare for his creation of character conveniently overlook the fact that these 'characters' would not exist without plot, for they are first and foremost agents and responsive victims of the story. It is a point made by Joan Rees in her book *Shakespeare and the Story* (1978). Stripped to its essence, comedy in Shakespearian terms is not judged just on laughs, or even on the existence of the central fact of love, but on a certain kind of plot which ends (with only one exception, *Love's Labour's Lost*) with the happy resolution of a love plot and the restoration of social harmony. Both types of resolution are achieved by the ending of *The Merry Wives*, and the play's source of laughter lies as much in the misunderstandings and manipulations practised along the way as in the unique set of 'characters' created by such an intricate and interrelated set of plots.

SCENIC FORM

Shakespeare was clearly very clever at co-ordinating a series of complex plots. However, in his time he was not self-evidently exceptional in this aspect of the playwright's art. If anything, his younger contemporary, Ben Jonson, was tighter and more economical, for Shakespeare had a propensity for loosely following his whim in apparently gratuitous directions. Act IV scene i, the scene in which young William is grilled on his Latin accidence, is a case in point. What does mark Shakespeare out is his extraordinary capacity to build a scene, not just as a function of the developing plot, but almost as an end in itself, as he milks every incident for its dramatic potential, plays upon audience expectations and responses, and purposefully creates an incidental climax or anticlimax to close the scene. He may have learned this aspect of his craft from his dramatic rival, Marlowe, and from his reading of prose romances such as Sidney's *Arcadia*, but if so he surpassed his models. Bertolt Brecht, the great twentieth-century playwright, spotted the importance of the technique of integrated, episodic structure based upon the scene, and incorporated it into his own 'epic drama'. Among critics, the person who has examined most directly what he calls 'scenic form' in Shakespeare's plays is Emrys Jones:

> Plays are made of scenes before they are made of words (although a play of Shakespeare's, like *Macbeth*, may be as great a poem as it is a play). The dramatist's first and proper task is to dramatize; and the scene is the primary dramatic unit, the unit in terms of which he will work out his play.

Almost any scene in *The Merry Wives* repays close study from this point of view, but one in particular is immensely effective on the stage and does not figure prominently elsewhere in this book (probably because its success is not located in language or 'themes' but in theatrical effects which are not so easy to capture on the page). This is III. iii, the scene which is central to the play in more ways than one, where Falstaff is carried out in a buck-basket while Ford searches the house in near-paranoia. In metadramatic fashion, the characters take into their own hands responsibility for the 'plotting' as if they need no dramatist, and the scene opens in urgent fashion in preparations:

Mistress Ford.	Marry, as I told you before, John and Robert, be ready here hard by in the brew-house. And when I suddenly call you, come forth, and, without any pause or staggering, take this basket on your shoulders. That done, trudge with it in all haste, and carry it among

	the whitsters in Datchet Mead, and
	there empty it in the muddy ditch
	close by the Thames side.
Mistress Page.	You will do it?
Mistress Ford.	I ha' told them over and over – they
	lack no direction. – Be gone, and come
	when you are called.

                        [Exeunt John and Robert]
        [Enter Robin]

                                    (III. iii. 8–19)

The boy Robin has been taken into the conspiracy, and he is one of the inconspicuous but not superfluous minor characters, such as the servants John and Robert, who all play their parts. Mistress Page hides and Falstaff unwittingly enters an ambush. He thinks the situation is a lovers' tryst with Mistress Ford, and there is a kind of dramatic aria as she encourages his advances. Robin, playing his part (as consciously as an actor is playing his own part) enters to warn Falstaff that Mistress Page has arrived 'sweating and blowing and looking wildly' (82–3). Falstaff hides from the 'tattling' woman, only to overhear her message that the jealous Ford is approaching 'with half Windsor at his heels' (107). She whips up the pace and the women urgently bundle Falstaff into the linen basket. Now the stage fills with the entrance of Ford, Page, Caius, Evans, John and Robert. It is something of a speciality of Shakespeare to create this kind of scene, beginning with just one or two individuals involved in what they think is an intimate occasion, and then gradually crowding the stage with as many people as he can. Falstaff is carried out unknown to Ford, and Ford's hysteria bubbles over and is roundly reproved by Page. The penitent Ford apologises in puzzled disarray, and promises dinner, and the scene subsides with the unconscious double meanings of the Welshman Evans and the Frenchman Caius, in inconsequential conversation, as the ensemble disperses. Shakespeare by this time has created what, to the characters, is an anticlimax, for it is only the women, having orchestrated it all, who know what is happening. To the men, it is an example of Ford's irrational temper, and is otherwise unexplained. A true climax is frustrated at this point, since Shakespeare wants to use the whole pattern again in IV. v when Falstaff is forced to disguise himself as the old woman of Brainford. In this way Shakespeare, while creating each scene with a careful eye to pacing, and while 'rhyming' two scenes with the same pattern (much to Ford's bafflement), saves up the true climax for the last scene. It is a way of making each scene a complete episode in itself, with its beginning, middle and end, while stitching it into what comes before and after and reserving the crescendo for the last section of the play. Act III scene iii is a scene much beloved of the operatic adapters whom we shall look at in a later chapter, and we can see why, with its strong, clear pattern controlled by the women and known by the audience, and with its scope for building up massive musical effects with so many characters on stage together, all in different states of awareness and unawareness, agitation and triumph. Verdi, apparently going out of his way to complicate things even further, was to add Anne and Fenton, hiding behind a screen in a clandestine lovers' meeting. It is also a scene much beloved of directors and audiences for its ripe opportunities for farce. In its own, underestimated way, it is one of the great scenes in Shakespeare, a wonderful example of his stagecraft exercised in his unique 'scenic form' for comic effect.

STRUCTURAL DISCONTINUITIES

So far I have drawn attention to structures which are in some sense part of a homogeneous and continuing pattern, unfolding with increasing complexity in almost self-generating fashion, while being scenically organised to arrest an audience's attention with a total concentration on the present moment. Equally characteristic of Shakespeare, and perhaps more puzzling at least to the modern eye, are the sudden shifts and changes which seem not to spring from the past and do not necessarily lead into the future. It is probably these incidents which have caused most bother to critics and directors since Shakespeare's day, and yet they happen so insistently in the plays that they cannot be ignored. Once again, comparison may be made with Brecht, who learned so much from Shakespeare. His own theories of *Verfremdungseffekt*, by which the audience is never allowed to settle into one level of illusion, are very similar to the practice of Shakespeare, although it is a moot point whether the effects are the same in each dramatist since Brecht is so much more consciously polemical.

Act iv scene i, the short scene with William reciting Latin to give opportunity for the unwitting malapropisms of Mistress Quickly, is an obvious example. It has no bearing on the plot whatsoever. There are explanations for its presence, and they are just as much 'structural' as the devices that splice episodes together and interconnect. The scene comes as a pastoral interlude after a distressed and distressing soliloquy from Ford in which he doubts his own sanity. It returns us to a sense of the diurnal normality of the town, a little holiday from the high drama, reminding us what the world of Windsor would be like without its interlopers, a world where little boys grow up slowly day by day under the nurturing if often irrelevant attentions of well-meaning schoolteachers, and reminding us also that we are in the world of comedy. It is a return to a norm of Windsor rhythms, just as symphonies must every now and then retrieve their key notes and their recurrent melodies, as a fulcrum amidst the rising and falling eddies and shallows of the music around them. And if Emrys Jones is right in another of his theories, that Shakespeare deliberately structures his plays in two parts separated by an interval, then iv. i clearly marks the break, the first part ending on a note of cliffhanging high emotion, the second, incidentally giving time for the audience to find their places and settle down, beginning on a quiet note before building up again towards the climax of the play.

Less easily explained is the climax itself, the entire shift of mode and characterisation in v. v. It is quite common in a Shakespeare play for the penultimate scenes to be somewhat flat dramatically, and they can be considered as an expedient readjustment of the plot, a putting-in-place of crucial plans, before the ensemble and divulgences of the ending. Even in a play which is universally admired such as *King Lear*, we find that before the final moments of the play there is some undistinguished writing and perhaps clumsy organisation. From IV. vi to v. iv of *The Merry Wives* we get a series of such scenes which are all very brief, significant only in that they clear the way for the ending, and having a perfunctory air about them. They do not, however, seriously distort the decorum of the play, for it has been largely conducted in prose and in prosaic arrangements, building up to comic climaxes.

What does seem strange are the sudden switches of tone in the last scene. It happens often in Shakespearian comedy – the creaky artifice of the masque of Hymen at the end of *As You Like It*, the relaxing of tension in *The Merchant of Venice* after the terrifying scene in the courtroom, the radical changes effected by the plays within plays at the end of *Love's Labour's Lost* and *A Midsummer Night's Dream*, and even the movement into ceremonial formality and simplistic resolution of the last scene in *Measure for Measure*. Among the most abrupt and disjunctive of such changes is the end of *The Merry Wives*.

The changes are manifold and radical. We move from day to midnight, from town to forest, from prose to the rhyming, chanting poetry that would sit more easily in the *Dream* than in this play. Falstaff is more or less the same, exhibiting as much his monumental ego and his word-crunching wit as the triumph of hope over experience in his expectations of the sexual delights in store for him as he awaits the two women. The women enter, seductively, as into his fantasy. But with the stage direction we get a seismic shift: 'Enter Evans as a Satyr, Mistress Quickly as the Queen of Fairies, Pistol as Hobgoblin, Anne Page and the boy as Fairies. They carry tapers'. Evans as Satyr? Mistress Quickly as the Queen of the Fairies? Pistol as Hobgoblin? No casting could be so incongruous, contradictory or fantastic. The words then spoken by Quickly, Pistol and Evans respectively are quite unlike anything they could be expected to say if we judge from their previous appearances – rhyming couplets and 'fairy talk'. What on earth is going on, and how is a modern director to cope with all this?

I have no cogent answers to these questions that satisfy even myself. There are things that can be said for the sake of form. Resolution of emotional problems in Shakespearian comedy often comes in the topsy-turvy 'green' world of forests or at night by taper-light, rather than in the humdrum daylight world of the town. There is a practical reason in some cases, for if a play was written for outdoor performance in the afternoon, the dramatist could take advantage of the waning light towards the end. This clearly happens in *Love's Labour's Lost*: 'A light for Monsieur Judas! It grows dark, he may stumble' (v. ii. 622). And in this context everything may change, including any stable sense of character. Or we might say that Shakespeare is consciously changing the whole mode of the play to achieve a new mood of mystery, transposing the irrationality of love and lust demonstrated in the play into a feeling of strangeness and heightened unreality. A director has an awkward and real choice to make about how to handle this scene, whether to go for the 'magic' or the sheer farce. Each may be effective and appropriate, but it is difficult to see the two coexisting. Perhaps Shakespeare genuinely intended new characters, and since his acting troupe was limited in numbers he simply used the names of those who had already appeared as a shorthand for the actors' convenience. Or we might conclude that Shakespeare is cynically manipulating plot, characterisation and audience, simply in order to evade the rather serious implications of a story that involves inflammatory issues such as lust, jealousy and revenge. So much is often said of the end of *Measure for Measure* – an expedient ruse to end an action comically that otherwise might lead to tears. But accept the changes we must, for there seems no genuine way to gloss over them and make of the artefact the kind of ceramic unity that critics like, or to readjust the critical focus so as to define some 'unifying principle', which will make everything cohere.

T. W. Craik, in the most recent single-volume edition of *The Merry Wives* (the Oxford Shakespeare, 1990), has analysed the ending in considerable detail, with an eye to its possible functions and effects. First, Craik argues, there is the twofold structural object, 'to finish off the main plot with the third assignation and Falstaff's final and public discomfiture' and 'to finish off the minor plot with Anne Page's marriage to Master Fenton' (pp. 20–1). I have implicitly questioned the notion of a hierarchy of plots ('main' and 'minor') in the polyphony of a Shakespearian comedy such as *The Merry Wives*, but the point about finalising plots is certainly true. Craik argues also that the shift into blank verse is to persuade us to 'suspend our disbelief for the sake of enjoying what will happen' (p. 22). Finally, the ending is seen as an elaborate vehicle for extending thinly veiled compliments to Queen Elizabeth. Not that the Fairy Queen is an allegory of Elizabeth, but the whole deployment of fairy characters would recall to a contemporary audience, Craik suggests, the most elaborate compliment of all, Spenser's *The Faerie Queene*. The 'delicate balance' (p. 24) maintained by Shakespeare allows the play to end on a note of forgiveness and reconciliation rather than revenge. Craik also indicates the theatrical potential of the ending, when he surveys performances. In Terry Hands' 1968 production, the ending was played with violence and with 'an undertone of real terror' (p. 44), as Falstaff is surrounded and tormented. Verdi's opera, which we shall look at later, can create a similar effect, and Hands may even have found the idea in the opera. We are also reminded in this context that Northrop Frye read the ending of the play as a ritual of the defeat and victimisation of a 'scapegoat', namely Falstaff, and such an idea might legitimise the effect of violence.

However, admirer as he is, Craik detects some 'incongruity' in the ending as a tonal conclusion to this play. We must simply accept this element, and there seems no real way to argue for ceramic unity of design or conception, or to readjust the critical focus so as to define some 'unifying principle' at work which will make everything neatly cohere. Shakespeare's fatal, but wonderful, habit of putting at risk overall unity by working in the medium of spectacular scenes, may be our last resort as an explanation.

Discontinuity and disjunction, the breaking of one illusion to step into another, are inescapable facts at least in Shakespeare's comedies and perhaps also in his tragedies. The ending of Brecht's *The Good Person of Szechwan* purposefully builds upon the contrivance of Shakespeare's comic closures, suggesting that they are constructed by audience expectations meeting with the dramatist's desire to surprise. Indeed, Brecht's whole theory of *Verfremdungseffekt* ('alienation effect') was forged from his intimate knowledge of Shakespeare's plays in all their radical discontinuities.

If there are answers to the question of what contemporary Elizabethan audiences made of such scenes in the context of plays as wholes, they lie buried within the Elizabethan stages on the Bankside beside the Thames in London. And even the recent unearthing of the foundations of the Rose and the Globe will not yield up such secrets.

· 4 ·

Language

The Merry Wives of Windsor was written in a particularly fertile period of England's linguistic development. Whereas Latin had been the internationally sanctioned language of literature and education right through the medieval and early Tudor periods, the English vernacular had gained new respect in Elizabeth I's reign, and during the 1580s and 1590s it came into its own with its adoption by the greatest writers. In the 1580s Edmund Spenser had shown an audacious confidence in the language by composing the first three books of the first epic poem in 'modern' English, *The Faerie Queene*. Sir Philip Sidney had written an epic romance in English prose, the *Arcadia*. Dramatists such as Marlowe, Kyd, Shakespeare, Lyly and Greene – those who are hailed as the greatest dramatists in the golden age of the English theatre – all turned their backs on the academic drama in Latin of their forebears and committed themselves to English as the vehicle for serious drama. Not only this, many writers, and in particular Lyly and Shakespeare, were virtually involved in establishing Latin as a 'colony' of English by taking over many words and constructions and 'anglicising' them.

Whole plays by Shakespeare reflect the general ferment of linguistic innovation, assimilation, and the fact of language's importance in Elizabethan England. *Love's Labour's Lost* focuses on taking responsibility for one's 'word' while also contrasting the flowery and the plain ways of speaking. In this and in fact in all his plays Shakespeare coins many new English words by drawing upon Latin roots. He also implies a moral preference for the 'russet yeas and honest kersey noes' (*Love's Labour's Lost*, v. ii. 412) of English over the Latinate, learned and ornate vocabulary and rhetoric used by characters like Don Armado, Sir Nathaniel and the schoolmaster Holofernes. In *The Merry Wives of Windsor* Shakespeare contributes to the debate about language in different ways. He shows the interaction of Latin and English explicitly in one scene. More significantly, we see him setting up a norm of English language which acts as an indicator of what is by contrast deviant. In doing so Shakespeare's practice may be seen as one of the forces that has strengthened the foundation which has underpinned imperialistic England's assumption of superiority over other races – those who speak with a foreign accent or with apparent affectation are different, funny, and sometimes wicked. At this level, language is not an exuberant sport but a weapon of power.

The most innocent level at which Shakespeare raises language to a directly dramatic level comes in the spectacularly irrelevant but charming scene which opens Act Four, where the boy William is put through his paces in Latin by Parson Evans. Shakespeare seems to have had a particular fondness for affectionately satirising country teachers, and it is not so fanciful a biographical speculation as some others that he is recalling his own schooldays in Stratford when he draws Holofernes and Evans. (It seems that Evans is William's schoolmaster and it is not clear why Slender has the power of declaring a holiday at iv. i. 12.) The affection comes through in the ways that these characters are made likeable and dignified even in their unselfconsciously pedantic excesses. Antony had enough respect for his modest schoolteacher to send him as emissary in defeat to Octavius Caesar, who regards the man as no more than 'so poor a pinion of [Antony's] wing', a sign of how the great general is 'pluck'd' (*Antony and Cleopatra*, III. xii. 2–6). So far as I know, the only recent scholar to take any interest in Shakespeare's own schoolteacher is E. A. J. Honigmann in *Shakespeare: The lost years*. It should of course be said in praise of Shakespeare's schoolmaster, and the Elizabethan educational system, that this particular pupil became probably the most astonishingly successful user of words who has ever lived. And his words were not just English ones, for despite the scornful comments of Ben Jonson and others on Shakespeare's 'small Latin and less Greek', his learning is considerable. Like the famous schoolteacher of his day, Richard Mulcaster, he could say, 'I honour the Latin but I worship the English'.

Act IV scene i is a scene which adds nothing to the plot (it appears in the Folio version but not at all in the Quarto), but contributes to the building up of the Windsor ethos which we have already looked at. It shows a benign side to the town, although young William may not see it as entirely generous that he should be tested rigorously in Latin on a day which has been declared a school holiday, a 'playing day' (IV. i. 10). It opens with his mother's and father's fear that William 'profits nothing in the world at his book' (IV. i. 15). William proves otherwise by showing his competence in Latin grammar and vocabulary. The real target of the satire is the unashamedly English woman, Mistress Quickly, who, knowing no Latin, constantly mishears the terms and Latin words as English ones: 'polecat' for *pulcher*, 'hang-hog' (bacon) for Evans' pronunciation of *hic, haec, hoc*. Her creative imagination runs riot with 'genitive' which becomes Jenny and *horum* which becomes whore. It may be too slight a scene to hang solemn interpretations upon, but one could point to Mistress Quickly's habit as one shared in more disastrous ways by others who create new meanings out of apparent mishearings (or by making sense of things which do not seem readily familiar) such as Othello, Lear and a host of other characters. One more layer of irony in the scene is at the expense of Parson Evans. He puts himself in the position of the examiner, but because of his Welsh accent his own rendering of Latin becomes idiosyncratic (*hig, hag, hog* for *hic, haec, hoc,* and *hung, hang, hog* for *hunc, hanc, hoc*). Young William comes through the experience with flying colours, having proved (in Evans's colourful term) his 'good sprag memory' (IV. i. 78). Mistress Quickly and Parson Evans are not so impressive in their learning, although in their different ways they have added a memorable set of Latin adoptions and adaptions into English.

The presentation of Evans' Welsh as eccentric alerts us to a more insistent and less innocent use of language as a subject in itself in *The Merry Wives.* Just as we could group the characters into virtuous, stable 'insiders' (or so they see themselves) and volatile, dangerous 'outsiders', so we can make a similar division along linguistic lines. With the exception of a few, insiders tend to speak normative English, straightforward and unadorned, while outsiders have amusing accents, or they speak in bizarre and aberrant ways. The only factor that complicates the linguistic as distinct from moral division is that some characters, in spite of their speech, prove themselves corrigible and able to become conforming insiders by accepting certain prevailing attitudes.

Page is regarded by many in Windsor as one who embodies the virtues held dear by this society. Before we meet him, we hear him described by Shallow as 'honest Master Page' (I. i. 61). There is textual evidence that Shakespeare originally called the character Thomas, but as if to eliminate any associations with doubting, he made him George – about as English as one could get. He is steady, sober, hospitable and thrifty, and unlike Ford he does not suspect his wife and he immediately apportions blame where it belongs – on Falstaff's impertinent letters. If he has shortcomings, such as his wish for Anne to marry into solid money rather than for love, and perhaps also a hint of complacency, they are simply consequences of what Windsor regards as virtues. His mode of speech is consistent with all his other attributes. When he enters, his words come as plain straightforwardness after the chatter of Shallow and Evans: 'I am glad to see your worships well. I thank you for my venison, Master Shallow' (I. i. 74–5). From this moment on he becomes a measure of unpretentious good sense showing up the 'affectations' and oddities of others around. He is also the conciliator, and uses meals as a way of bringing people together, inviting even the reprobate Falstaff:

> Wife, bid these gentlemen welcome. Come, we have a hot venison pasty to dinner. Come, gentlemen, I hope we shall drink down all unkindness.
>
> (I. i. 180–2)

After learning of Falstaff's designs on his wife, he is loftily indignant: 'I never heard such a drawling, affecting rogue' (II. i. 132). It is noteworthy that this condemnation is directed mainly at Falstaff's affected style rather than his actions, and indeed Page seems to equate bad language with bad living: 'Here's a fellow frights English out of his wits' (II. i. 129–30). In a different context, Falstaff himself, in a pun, acknowledges the difference between his own and Page's economic, moral and linguistic worlds:

> No quips now, Pistol. Indeed, I am in the waist two yards about. But I am now about no waste – I am about thrift. Briefly, I do mean to make love to Ford's wife. I spy entertainment in her. She discourses, she carves, she gives the leer of invitation. I can construe the action of her familiar style; and the hardest voice of her behaviour – to be Englished rightly – is 'I am sir John Falstaff's'.
>
> (I. iii. 37–44)

Falstaff's life has been one of conspicuous waste (just as his waist is his most conspicuous physical attribute), while Page's life has been one of thrift. Falstaff is not really planning to change his life but instead to use a different tactic in wooing Ford's wife. What is remarkable in his speech is the central reference point of language. After 'thrift' he *speaks* 'briefly'. Then he digresses into excess again, but draws himself back into the Windsor ethos with 'the familiar *style*' of Mistress Ford, gives her 'the hardest *voice* of her behaviour' which, 'to be *Englished* rightly' is a terse phrase ' "I am Sir John Falstaff's" ' (my italics). He may be wrong in his interpretation of the woman's behaviour, but his analysis is interesting because he relentlessly harps on an assumption that would surely be shared by Page, that the use of language is an ethical practice in which 'thrift' may be as important as it is in daily economy. The debate between the florid and the plain seems to have been a lifelong preoccupation of Shakespeare's. Throughout his plays, the plain is often associated with honesty which can be unimaginative and sometimes, as in Cordelia's 'Nothing', brutal, while the florid is associated with generosity, imagination and entertainment.

No other character is quite so eloquently plain in this play as Page. Slender is economical in his language out of tongue-tied shyness when addressing Anne Page, but he can be relatively verbose when he is telling her about his servants. He knows exactly how much was in his pocket when, he alleges, Pistol picked it:

> Ay, by these gloves, did he – or I would I might never come in mine own great chamber again else – of seven groats in mill-sixpences, and two Edward shovel-boards, that cost me two shillings and twopence apiece of Yed Miller, by these gloves.
>
> (I. i. 142–6)

The boastfulness involved in letting slip incidentally that he has a 'great chamber' is a recurrent note of Slender's. He has his moments of sentimentality when falling in love, and at the same time imperiousness towards his servant:

> I had rather than forty shillings I had my Book of Songs and Sonnets here.
> [Enter Simple]
> How now, Simple, where have you been? I must wait on myself, must I? You have not the Book of Riddles about you, have you?

Simple's reply has the Windsor ring of specific detail about time and place:

> Book of Riddles? Why, did you not lend it to Alice Shortcake upon Allhallowmas last, a fortnight afore Michelmas?
>
> (I. i. 183–90)

Like some other conversations in the play, it goes nowhere, serving mainly to build up the atmosphere of this somewhat slow town. Simple's reply is one of his longest speeches, and usually he restricts himself, like the other servant John Rugby, to phrases like 'Well, sir', 'I'll go watch', and 'Here, sir'.

Ford's 'normal' speech is analogous to Page's ('if I find her honest, I lose not my labour'), but when tricking Falstaff he can match the knight's circumlocutory flattery:

> . . . you are a gentleman of excellent breeding, admirable discourse, of great admittance, authentic in your place and person, generally allowed for your many, warlike courtlike, and learned preparations.
>
> (II. ii. 217–21)

His being disguised, and his acting deviously, makes his language – at least in Windsor – more suspect. When roused to jealous fury he finds a voice which uses rhetorical devices and almost poetic rhythms, although without the spacious worldliness of reference adopted by Falstaff, and with more than a hint of racism:

> I will rather trust a Fleming with my butter, Parson Hugh the Welshman with my cheese, an Irishman with my aqua-vitae bottle, or a thief to walk my ambling gelding, than my wife with herself. Then she plots, then she ruminates, then she devises.
>
> (II. ii. 286–91)

It would seem that in Ford's case language is a measure of deviation from straightforward honesty and trust.

If there are speakers who, while retaining integrity, adopt

a golden mean between complete lack of adornment and wild embellishment, they are the women. Mistresses Page and Ford and also Anne Page adopt a straightforward speech practice in which they manage to say exactly what they mean without being prosaic or dull. Indignation rather than the desire to embellish plain thoughts governs their use of rhetoric and images:

Mistress Page.	. . . For revenged I will be, as sure as his guts are made of puddings.
	(II. i. 28–9)
Mistress Ford.	. . . What tempest, I trow, threw this whale, with so many tuns of oil in his belly, ashore at Windsor?
	(II. i. 59–60)
Anne Page.	[On the prospect of marrying Caius] Alas, I had rather be set quick i'th'earth, And bowled to death with turnips.
	(III. iv. 84–5)

Apart from such vigorous flights of metaphorical fancy, the language of these morally central women is generally functional, clear and direct. If their actions are not so straightforward, it is because they are driven to stratagems by the men.

What complicates any linguistic analysis which equates Windsorites with the plain style and outsiders with excess is that some who fall in the former group do have 'dialects' of their own. Evans is the prime example of one who has presumably been tamed into Windsor orthodoxy and gained acceptance in spite of his being Welsh. Although Falstaff is continually infuriated by Evans' capacity to make 'fritters of English' (v. v. 142) with terms like 'seese' (cheese) and 'putter' (butter), and with his pribbles and prabbles, Evans has been completely accepted into Windsor society. He even speaks for the society, with fine alliteration and symmetries for effect, in condemnation of those like Falstaff who are '. . . given to fornications, and to taverns, and sack, and wine, and metheglins, and to drinkings, and swearings and starings, pribbles and prabbles' (v. v. 156–8). Language is apparently not a permanent barrier in this version of little England, and verbal eccentricity can be tolerated so long as dominant, behavioural mores are observed. Even the highest in the society, Justice Shallow, is marked by a language which is distinctive, and is derived from his legal training and early experiences at the Inns of Court in London. He opens with legal terms, declaring his status as Justice of the Peace and Coram (a special justice) at that, speaking of Ratalorum and Armigero, 'bill, warrant, quittance or obligation' (i. i. 8–10). Later, inspired by the impending duel between Evans and Caius, he reveals another specialist vocabulary, that of the vigorous blade fighting duels, while lamenting the modern terminology of the sport:

> In these times you stand on distance, your passes, stoccadoes, and I know not what. 'Tis the heart, Master Page; 'tis here, 'tis here. I have seen the time, with my long sword, I would have made you four tall fellows skip like rats.
>
> (ii. i. 206–11)

What is really particularised about Shallow's speech is not an unusual or arcane vocabulary but a brisk and clipped rhythm, a tendency to repeat phrases like ''Tis your fault, 'tis your fault' (i. i. 88) and to use as expletives terms like 'By yea and nay'.

The Host of the Garter is another character who, while being thoroughly local in his outlook, has a colourful idiom. He is bluff and hearty, greeting Caius with 'Bless thee, bully doctor' (ii. iii. 6), and he is one who is a master of the linguistic joke that exploits the foreigner's ignorance of English colloquialisms:

Host.   . . . A word, Mounseur Mockwater.
Caius.   Mockvater? Vat is dat?
Host.   Mockwater, in our English tongue, is valour, bully.

Caius.	By gar, then I have as much mockvater as de Englishman. Scurvy jack-dog priest! By gar, me vill cut his ears.
Host.	He will clapper-claw thee tightly, bully.
Caius.	Clapper-de-claw? Vat is dat?
Host.	That is, he will make thee amends.
Caius.	By gar, me do look he shall clapper-de-claw me, for, by gar, me vill have it.

(II. iii. 52–63)

The source of the audience's amusement here is twofold, both sides hinging on a distinction between insiders and outsiders. First, we laugh at the Host's manipulation of the guileless Caius who must accept what he is told about English, knowing no better. Secondly, we laugh directly *at* Caius' accent which immediately types him as Franco-German. In both cases what fuels the comedy is our own assumption, easily complicit with the Host, about the linguistic superiority of English. The Host is one of the most versatile speakers and he can adopt a bombastic mock-classicism for purposes of hearty humour, again at the expense of Caius:

Caius.	Vat be you all, one, two, tree, four, come for?
Host.	To see thee fight, to see thee foin, to see thee traverse, to see thee here, to see thee there, to see thee pass thy punto, thy stock, thy reverse, thy distance, thy montant. Is he dead, my Ethiopian? Is he dead, my Francisco? Ha, bully? What says my Aesculapius? My Galen? My heart of elder? Ha? Is he dead, bully stale? Is he dead?
Caius.	By gar, he is de coward Jack priest of de vorld. He is not show his face.
Host.	Thou art a Castalion-King-Urinal. Hector of Greece, my boy!

(II. iii. 20–31)

Some of the Host's epithets here send up the doctor with

their extravagant grandiosity while others are subtle insults, and the Host can maintain his tone because of the gap in linguistic competence between himself and Caius. The Host's tone suits his job, which requires a certain chameleon-like quality in persuading people that he is flattering them while in fact he is making sure the rent is paid. He is ruthless in his advice to Falstaff to dismiss his men and, mistrusting Falstaff's promises of money, he employs Bardolph as barman. Both are ploys to ensure he gets his rent, and he carries them out with *bonhomie* and even gusto:

> *Falstaff.* Mine host of the Garter –
>
> *Host.* What says my bully rook? Speak scholarly and wisely.
>
> *Falstaff.* Truly, mine host, I must turn away some of my followers.
>
> *Host.* Discard, bully Hercules, cashier. Let them wag; trot, trot.
>
> *Falstaff.* I sit at ten pounds a week.
>
> *Host.* Thou'rt an emperor – Caesar, Keisar, and Pheazar. I will entertain Bardolph; he shall draw, he shall tap. Said I well, bully Hector?
>
> *Falstaff.* Do so, good mine host.
>
> *Host.* I have spoke. Let him follow. [To Bardolph] Let me see thee froth and lime. I am at a word. Follow.
>
> (i. iii. 1–14)

Just as the Host manipulates the plot, he can adroitly manipulate language to get his own way without ever arousing the ire or suspicion of those he is addressing. In acting as a *deus in machina* (or dramatist within the play) to avoid bloodshed between Evans and Caius, he explains his motives in linguistic terms:

> Disarm them, and let them question. Let them keep their limbs whole and hack our English.
>
> (iii. i. 70–1)

Linguistically, as in other ways, Mistress Quickly provides a curious case. Like Justice Shallow, she is one of the characters Shakespeare imports from the Henriad, where she had been Hostess of the Boar's Head in Cheapside, and (now married to Pistol) among the mourners after the death of Falstaff. In *The Merry Wives* we have seen the inception of Pistol's affection for her (ii. ii. 131–4), which may even imply that Shakespeare is setting this play *before* the Henry plays and allowing her to follow Falstaff back to London. Be this as it may, she has a different context of living in Windsor. She is Doctor Caius' housekeeper. She is also confidante to Anne Page in ways that make it easy to assume a long acquaintance since Anne's childhood. Her role can easily be seen as comparable to Juliet's Nurse, and her language encourages such a speculation:

Fenton.	What news? How does pretty Mistress Anne?
Mistress Quickly.	In truth, sir, and she is pretty, and honest, and gentle – and one that is your friend. I can tell you that by the way, I praise heaven for it.
Fenton.	Shall I do any good, thinkest thou? Shall I not lose my suit?
Mistress Quickly.	Troth, sir, all is in His hands above. But notwithstanding, Master Fenton, I'll be sworn on a book she loves you. Have not your worship a wart above your eye?
Fenton.	Yes, marry, have I. What of that?
Mistress Quickly.	Well, thereby hangs a tale. Good faith, it is such another Nan – but, I detest, an honest maid as ever broke bread. We had an hour's talk of that wart. I shall never laugh but in that maid's company. But, indeed, she is given too much to allicholy and musing.

(i. iv. 133–49)

This will ring bells for those who recall the Nurse in *Romeo and Juliet*, since Mistress Quickly's language has the same incongruous mixture of sycophancy, platitudinousness ('I'll be sworn on a book she loves you'), confused words, abrupt inconsequentiality ('Have not your worship a wart above your eye?') and a tendency to be distracted from a train of thought. But this is only a part of her linguistic make-up. Mistress Quickly seems also to have been resident in Windsor in Mistress Ford's salad days when she was courted by a bevy of nobles from London, and she describes the scene with a vivacity that brings its own silken texture despite the malapropisms:

Falstaff.	Well, Mistress Ford – what of her?
Mistress Quickly.	Why, sir, she's a good creature. Lord, Lord, your worship's a wanton! Well, God forgive you, and all of us, I pray –
Falstaff.	Mistress Ford – come, Mistress Ford.
Mistress Quickly.	Marry, this is the short and the long of it: you have brought her into such a canaries as 'tis wonderful. The best courtier of them all, when the court lay at Windsor, could never have brought her to such a canary; yet there has been knights, and lords, and gentlemen, with their coaches, I warrant you, coach after coach, letter after letter, gift after gift, smelling so sweetly – all musk – and so rushling, I warrant you, in silk and gold, and in such alligant terms, and in such wine and sugar of the best and the fairest, that would have won any woman's heart, and, I warrant you, they could never get an eye-wink of her

> – I had myself twenty angels given
> me this morning, but I defy all
> angels in any such sort, as they say,
> but in the way of honesty – and, I
> warrant you, they could never get
> her so much as sip on a cup with the
> proudest of them all, and yet there
> has been earls – nay, which is more,
> pensioners – but, I warrant you, all
> is one with her.
>
> (II. ii. 53–75)

A cynic might well see this monologue as an elaborate and
sly suggestion to Falstaff that what Quickly wants from him
is 'angels' (coins) before she will say more, but an admirer of
Shakespeare could claim this passage as one of the greatest
examples of his dramatic prose with its inflected beauty,
calculated repetitions and orchestration of ongoing rhythm
riding over holding-phrases like 'I warrant you'. For a
minute her speech opens up a vignette of a glorious past of
Windsor itself which, one feels, casts its comforting glow of
nostalgia over the other backward-looking character, Shallow. What she says is all quite possibly fiction, and certainly
exaggeration, but glorious in its rich texture. In another
mode altogether, Mistress Quickly appears at the end of the
play – quite inexplicably – as Queen of the Fairies. Her
language here is reminiscent of *A Midsummer Night's
Dream*, in kind if not in quality:

> And nightly, meadow-fairies, look you sing,
> Like to the Garter's compass, in a ring.
> Th'expressure that it bears, green let it be,
> More fertile-fresh than all the field to see;
> And *Honi soit qui mal y pense* write
> In emerald tufts, flowers purple, blue, and white,
> Like sapphire, pearl, and rich embroidery,
> Buckled below fair knighthood's bending knee.
> Fairies use flowers for their charactery.
> Away, disperse! But till 'tis one o'clock,

Our dance of custom round about the oak
Of Herne the Hunter let us not forget.

(v. v. 65–76)

She recalls also the Witches in *Macbeth* in the punitive chant over Falstaff:

Fie on sinful fantasy!
Fie on lust and luxury!
Lust is but a bloody fire,
Kindled with unchaste desire,
Fed in heart, whose flames aspire,
As thoughts do blow them, higher and higher.
Pinch him, fairies, mutually,
Pinch him for his villainy.
Pinch him, and burn him, and turn him about,
Till candles and starlight and moonshine be out.

(v. v. 93–102)

The driving, vindictive pulses of the rhythms here are different again from the delicate lyricism of the earlier fairy tones. This localised kind of discontinuity or variation is not at all unusual in Shakespeare, who does not seem to have been so obsessed with consistency of 'characterisation' as the modern age has been. Indeed, the chants at the end accompanying Quickly are delivered by, of all people, Pistol and Evans, though without their special tricks of language. This may strictly speaking be a necessity of doubling of actors rather than implying the same 'characters'. But taking the evidence as a whole, we must conclude that Mistress Quickly's language does not add up to a single, stable or consistent 'character'. She is as much a mistress of Shakespearian verse as prose (and we should remember that verse is rare in this play, and is virtually confined to Fenton and Quickly and the songs at the end), and she recalls different plays in Shakespeare's output. We can only say that as a character she is discontinuous, a function of plot, a go-between, and a curiously orphic voice going between some of Shakespeare's most memorable dramatic speech-patterns in several plays, just as socially she goes between all classes.

These are the Windsorites, the 'insiders', and the problematical case of Mistress Quickly aside, they all use language which accepts certain tones which are normative and knowing. They are either plain-speakers, assimilated within Windsor despite speech-eccentricities, or superior to outsiders. The outsiders, whether knowingly or not, completely violate norms of behaviour and of speech.

There may be some moral virtue in speaking in plain, unadorned prose, or in docilely accommodating a foreign temperament to local norms. For a dramatist, however, these can be tame advantages when compared with the fun to be had with those who accept and flaunt their differences.

We have already seen this in the case of the hapless Doctor Caius, at sea linguistically as much as socially in the world of Windsor. He seems to have come to England either to practise medicine or find a wealthy woman to wed, or probably both. The status-conscious Mistress Quickly says he is 'well moneyed, and his friends Potent at court' (IV. iv. 86–7). His language is a broken mixture of English, German and French:

> Vat is you sing? I do not like dese toys. Pray you go and vetch me in my closet *un boîtier vert* – a box, a green-a box. Do intend vat I speak? A green-a box.
>
> (I. iv. 43–5)

He is a splenetic and impetuous character, as his landlady Mistress Quickly knows, and generally speaking he is neither likeable nor well-liked. It is possible that in time he could become accepted in the way Evans has been, particularly since he offers the skill of a doctor, but his amatory assault on Anne Page classes him among the threatening outsiders. It is in drawing Caius that Shakespeare comes closest in the play to the racist, imperialist stance of extracting humour from anybody who does not speak English, as if they are intrinsically funny. It is an assumption which, unfortunately, has taken root in the culture down to the present day, and which, in modern multicultural societies, should be questioned.

Fenton is another outsider in both class and language terms. A nobleman whose funds are presumably running out in an initially urgent task of seeking a moneyed wife from the provinces, he betrays his class origins, as we have already noted, in his use of poetic blank verse in a society where the closest anybody gets to poetry is reciting trite love songs from the Book of Songs and Sonnets (III. i. 10–30), at least until there is talk of the legend of Herne the Hunter (from IV. iv. 25 onwards). Fenton is suavely self-assured, and – in equal measure to his worldliness – suspected by the middle-class inhabitants of Windsor. There is even an oblique link between him and Falstaff, since he is rumoured to have been a fellow of the wild Prince Hal and Poins, as was Falstaff.

Falstaff and his men are most explicitly defined by their particular modes of speaking. Their opening argument with the locals is as much a contest of languages as of matter, as Falstaff brushes aside Evans' gesture of peace with an abrupt insult:

Evans.	*Pauca verba*, Sir John, good worts.
Falstaff.	Good worts? Good cabbage! – Slender, I broke your head. What matter have you against me?
Slender.	Marry, sir, I have matter in my head against you, and against your cony-catching rascals, Bardolph, Nym, and Pistol. They carried me to the tavern, and made me drunk, and afterward picked my pocket.
Bardolph.	You Banbury cheese!
Slender.	Ay, it is no matter.
Pistol.	How now, Mephostophilus?
Slender.	Ay, it is no matter.
Nym.	Slice, I say. *Pauca pauca*. Slice! That's my humour.

(I. i. 114–25)

Nym and Bardolph apparently physically threaten Slender ('Slice!') who meekly withdraws his accusations, but just as aggressive as actions is their abusive language. Bardolph's 'Banbury cheese!' is said to be a reference to Slender's thinness, but it sounds also like the arrogant, metropolitan person's contempt for the provincial. Bardolph's own great trademark is his red nose, a fact which allows Slender to retaliate with an insult (I. i. 157). Bardolph is the most taciturn of the three. Nym's 'That's my humour' is one of his own catch-phrases and marks him out as pretentious in his language. Evans gets his own back very quickly:

Falstaff.	Pistol!
Pistol.	He hears with ears.
Evans.	The tevil and his tam! What phrase is this, 'He hears with ear'? Why, it is affectations.

(I. i. 137–40)

It may be 'affectations' to the Welshman's ears, but it is the characteristic language of Nym, for every time he opens his mouth in the play it is to utter the word 'humour':

	I like not the humour of lying. He hath wronged me in some humours. I should have borne the humoured letter to her, but I have a sword and it shall bite upon my necessity. He loves your wife. There's the short and the long. My name is Corporal Nym. I speak, and I avouch 'tis true. My name is Nym, and Falstaff loves your wife. Adieu. I love not the humour of bread and cheese – and there's the humour of it. Adieu.
Page.	'The humour of it', quoth 'a! Here's a fellow frights English out of his wits.

(II. i. 120–30)

Again, there may be a hint of the urbanite's preference for repeated jargon in any age ('naff', 'streetwise', and so on). Bardolph has something of the same reliance on street slang of the city – 'And being fap, sir, was, as they say, cashiered'

(I. i. 164). Pistol prides himself on his classical references, usually of military extraction, and he is the most talkative and aggressive of the three:

> Shall I Sir Pandarus of Troy become—
> And by my side wear steel? Then Lucifer take all!
>
> (I. iii. 70–1)

> Thou art the Mars of malcontents. I second thee.
>
> (I. iii. 95)

> Ford.   Love my wife?
> Pistol.   With liver burning hot. Prevent. Or go thou
>   Like Sir Actaeon he, with Ringwood at thy
>   heels.
>
> (II. i. 109–11)

> [To Bardolph, just employed as tapster]
> O base Hungarian wight! Wilt thou the spigot
> wield?
>
> (I. iii. 19)

The disreputable three down from London regard Windsor with hostility, and their language is a signal of their outsider status.

When dealing with Falstaff, we must begin by distancing the character in *The Merry Wives* from the one of the same name in the *Henry* plays. Or alternatively, we may assume he is the same 'character' in a very different context and situation. In *Henry IV*, Parts One and Two, Falstaff is undisputed king of the Boar's Head Tavern, and his comically mannerist language is shown in full authority over others. He bends everything to a pun or witticism through an impervious and magisterial control which is as much over language itself as over those around him. Even the future King of England, Prince Hal, cannot command the same powerful and indomitable stance. His vivacity may be more prominent in Part One than in Part Two (where he is hounded by justice and by death consciousness), but in both plays he assumes a commanding authority which is moral (in its very amorality), witty and linguistic. In Windsor, on the other hand, Falstaff is rarely allowed to be even at his ease, let alone in control. From the outset he is given no social place and he is regarded as an unwelcome trouble-maker. His imperiousness here is received as mischief-making impertinence:

> *Falstaff.* Now, Master Shallow, you'll complain of me to the King?
> *Shallow.* Knight, you have beaten my men, killed my deer, and broke open my lodge.
> *Falstaff.* But not kissed your keeper's daughter?
>
> (I. i. 103–7)

Since we enter the story after some history of problems between Falstaff and Windsor, we may assume that he has already taken the measure of the local community. The real problem he faces in them is a complete lack of a sense of humour. Only the Host is capable of making jokes that Falstaff can appreciate (though with him Falstaff has to be rather exaggeratedly polite since he owes him money), and the women's humour is not with him but against him. In response to this unfavourable climate, Falstaff seems to have adopted an aggressive, drily sarcastic humour, since the robust wit of Cheapside is lost here. To make things even worse for himself, he alienates even his built-in, appreciative audience, Pistol and Nym, by arguing with them and finally dismissing them from service. Isolated from his natural milieu, he is a much diminished figure. This is almost certainly what has disappointed critics over the generations, but we should be aware that it is the context in which Falstaff has placed himself that makes his famous wit inappropriate and ineffectual, rather than that his loss of wit signals the decline of his own capacities, or of Shakespeare's capacities to write with the Falstaffian style. If there is a major joke about the play, it is this very inappropriateness, which Shakespeare highlights. He seemed to be inveterately curious about seeing how people would react to circum-stances which do not allow their strengths to flower – for example, when pitting against each other Isabella and Angelo in *Measure for Measure* in circumstances which are beyond their capacities to handle, or placing Othello the warrior in domestic marriage, or for that matter placing his undoubtedly wittiest hero in a corrupt court in Elsinore after the murder of his father and hasty remarriage of his mother to the murderer.

Significantly, when Falstaff himself has been humiliated by the women, and his ego bruised by a dunking in the Thames in a laundry-basket, he rises through indignation to something like his characteristic note:

Falstaff.	Bardolph, I say!
Bardolph.	Here, sir.
Falstaff.	Go fetch me a quart of sack – put a toast in't.

[Exit Bardolph]

Have I lived to be carried in a basket like a barrow of butcher's offal? And to be thrown in the Thames? Well, if I be served such another trick, I'll have my brains ta'en out and buttered, and give them to a dog for a new-year's gift. The rogues slighted me into the river with as little remorse as they would have drowned a blind bitch's puppies, fifteen i'th'litter. And you may know by my size that I have a kind of alacrity in sinking. If the bottom were as deep as hell, I should down. I had been drowned but that the shore was shelvy and shallow – a death that I abhor, for the water swells a man, and what a thing should I have been when I had been swelled! I should have been a mountain of mummy.

[Enter Bardolph with sack]

Bardolph.	Here's Mistress Quickly, sir, to speak with you.
Falstaff.	Come, let me pour in some sack to the Thames water, for my belly's as cold as if I had swallowed snow-balls to cool the reins. Call her in.
Bardolph.	Come in, woman.
	[Enter Mistress Quickly]
Mistress Quickly.	By your leave; I cry you mercy. Give your worship good morrow.
Falstaff.	Take away these chalices. Go, brew me a pottle of sack finely.
Bardolph.	With eggs, sir?
Falstaff.	Simple of itself. I'll no pullet-sperm in my brewage.

(III. v. 1–29)

He is as eloquent on the subject of the laundry into which he was shoved, 'with stinking clothes that fretted in their own grease. Think of that, a man of my kidney – think of that – that am as subject to heat as butter; a man of continual dissolution and thaw' (III. v. 103–6). Falstaff allows himself here his old habit of transcending circumstances with sheer rhetoric. Obesity can be translated into 'a kind of alacrity in sinking', greater swelling into 'a mountain of mummy' and an egg into 'pullet-sperm' (weirdly anticipating W. C. Field's famous phrase about water – 'Never touch the stuff – fish fuck in it'). Through euphemism and rhetoric, liabilities can be wittily turned into strengths. On another brief occasion we see him in rhetorical command of a situation, when wooing Mistress Ford, and here the velvety seductive-ness of court language is used even as it is being ostensibly rejected:

Come, I cannot cog and say thou art this and that, like a many of these lisping hawthorn-buds that come like women in men's apparel and smell like Bucklersbury in simple-time. I cannot. But I love thee, none but thee; and thou deservest it.

(III. iii. 65–70)

The only other time in this play Falstaff is allowed this kind of freedom to exercise his generous, myth-making capacities is when he enters Windsor Forest disguised as a male deer, intending to be hunted by the women:

> For me, I am here a Windsor stag, and the fattest, I think, i'th'forest. Send me a cool rut-time, Jove, or who can blame me to piss my tallow? – Who comes here? My doe?

[Enter Mistress Ford and Mistress Page]

Mistress Ford.   Sir John! Art thou there, my deer, my male deer?

Falstaff.   My doe with the black scut! Let the sky rain potatoes. Let it thunder to the tune of 'Greensleeves', hail kissing-comfits, and snow eringoes. Let there come a tempest of provocation, I will shelter me here.

[He embraces Mistress Ford]

Mistress Ford.   Mistress Page is come with me, sweetheart.

Falstaff.   Divide me like a bribed buck, each a haunch. I will keep my sides to myself, my shoulders for the fellow of this walk, and my horns I bequeath your husbands . . .

(v. v. 12–27)

If the play was written to show 'Sir John in love', now is the moment when we see him at his best, turning his huge size into a virtue, flaunting excess to the extent that two women may be generously served. The freedom of his wit is able to range more widely. Alas, the moment does not last, and there are precious few others like it in the play.

Before leaving the subject of language, it would be misleading not to mention that the whole subject – the way in which we should speak about language in literature – is matter for raging dispute at the moment among literary theoreticians.

The debate has always been carried on, but usually in philosophy, linguistics and even theology, and periodically it feeds into literary criticism. There are various ways of describing the issue at stake. What seems to be agreed now is that language can no longer be regarded as a transparent medium for a stable, preordained 'meaning'. Language is seen far more as a code or a system of signs, which can have autonomous existence and whose relation to 'meaning' or 'reality' is highly problematical. The medium itself, language as a virtually self-sufficient system which creates meaning, has replaced language as a way of conveying or communicating meaning. This is presumably why, to our surprise, even our most carefully worded statements are sometimes interpreted in ways beyond our expectations – as if words once uttered have an existence of their own irrespective of our intentions when using them, and irrespective of what 'reality' we are trying to convey. It is as if we live in a world of signifiers which have unconstrained or 'free' play, rather than living among 'things' which can be accurately and unambiguously signified.

At first such a conclusion causes dismay. It seems that we can never say what we mean or mean what we say. But it need not be so frightening, and indeed it may begin to explain for us the awesome power of language as well as the unexpected subtleties of communication. Shakespeare himself seems to have known of the phenomenon we are now analysing. Feste in *Twelfth Night* pretends to lament the demise of stable meanings, and yet his job as witty fool depends on puns and ambiguities and the whole repertoire of language's instability:

> To see this age! A sentence is but a chev'ril glove to a good wit. How quickly the wrong side may be turn'd outward! ... I can yield you [no reason] without words, and words are grown so false I am loath to prove reason with them.
>
> (III. i. 10–12 and 21–2)

Feste quite cleverly defines the nature of our problem – how can we ever 'prove' that language is logical if the only way we can conduct a 'proof' is in language itself? We cannot get out of its closed system into some kind of 'metalanguage' in which to debate the questions.

We need not go into the deeper recesses of this conundrum here. Luckily, we can sidestep it, or perhaps even solve it, by looking not so much at what is in the mind of the speaker/writer but what is in the mind of the hearer/reader, and it is this theoretical position which has been implicitly adopted in this book. A clue lies in a sentence in *Love's Labour's Lost*:

> A jest's prosperity lies in the ear
> Of him that hears it, never in the tongue
> Of him that makes it.
>
> (v. ii. 849–51)

More important than what the writer or actor intends to convey by his words is the way those words are received. A 'joke' turning on racial or gender difference may be greeted with hilarity by one person, with anger by another. Words that delight one person can hurt another. Time and again we find in *The Merry Wives* people responding in different ways, and what makes the wives laugh makes Ford suspicious and Falstaff wince. What irritates or humiliates characters can make us laugh or make us think. In similar ways, any audience or critic is making meaning out of the language given by the dramatist in a process of re-creation. And in a very real sense when we talk about 'character' we are talking about language, for these characters exist first as nothing but language and secondly only in so far as we are prepared to 'take what they mistake' and let 'imagination amend them' (in the words of Theseus in *A Midsummer Night's Dream*, v. i. 90 and 211). The play's prosperity lies in the ears of those who hear it: without responsive audiences and readers there would be no play and without the play the English language would be impoverished. The play, if nothing else, opens up as a subject in itself the exhilaration of language used with innovative freedom at a time of special fertility in the development of English.

Operatic adaptations of
The Merry Wives of Windsor

Throughout this book, I have tried not to assert what the play 'means', but rather what it *can* mean, in the belief that there are an infinite number of interpretations which can be generated from 'the words on the page', none of which precludes others. Editors 'realise' one potential within the words by making choices among possible textual variants. Readers will make interpretations which depend on their own personalities and preconceptions; directors and actors make real the words in a different and equally unique sense, while audiences then perform a further act of making individual and collective meanings out of the action presented on the stage. Interpretation is always an act of creation, or at least re-creation, and an activating of one set of potential patterns and significances at the expense of an infinite number of others. In this sense, those who seek to translate Shakespeare's plays into another mode, for example, opera, are engaged in an activity which, though it may demand more energy than just reading or watching the play, is not significantly different in kind from that exercised by the editor, reader, director, actors or audience. An opera based on one of Shakespeare's plays is obviously an inspired creation in its own right, but it is also a re-creation of the original, just as most of Shakespeare's plays (but apparently not *The Merry Wives*) are adaptations, imitations or recreations of older works into material for the stage. The composer and librettist of an opera, then, can comment as effectively on the play as any critic, simply by making a selection of what seems important and drawing out one potential set of emphases from the given 'text'. The central doctrine of the Renaissance, the concept of 'imitation', is in essence precisely this. For this reason, I wish now to widen the perspective to include some 'imitations', great works of art based on *The Merry Wives of Windsor*, operas which themselves have stood the test of time. Since the composers were, respectively, Prussian, Italian and English, it is also timely to remind ourselves of the creativity of translation which has taken Shakespeare out of the hands of the English-speaking world and made his plays internationally accessible.

It may come as a surprise that there have been ten operas (one incomplete) based on Shakespeare's *The Merry Wives of Windsor*. The only plays which have inspired more operas are *The Tempest* (31), *Romeo and Juliet* (24), *Hamlet* (14), *A Midsummer Night's Dream* (14), *The Taming of the Shrew* (11) and *The Merchant of Venice* (11). The dates of composition for the various *Merry Wives* operas show a spread over time – 1761, 1773, 1794, 1796, 1799, 1838, 1849, 1856, 1893 and 1929. Only two, however, have gained continuing celebrity. Otto Nicolai's *The Merry Wives of Windsor* (*Die Lustigen Weiber von Windsor*) of 1849 is not often performed as a whole, but its overture and certain arias are popular concert pieces. Verdi's *Falstaff* (1893) with its libretto by Boito is, of course, hailed as one of the very greatest comic operas and is often performed. I shall be dealing with these two, and with one more, Vaughan Williams' *Sir John in Love* (1929), which is not ranked highly by musicologists and which has not been in circulation on record in its entirety for some time. Brief comments on the others may be found in Winton Dean's chapter in the invaluable book *Shakespeare in Music*, edited by Phyllis Hartnoll (London, 1964). There are, of course, many more specialised books on the music.

My interest lies not so much in the music as such (mainly because I cannot pretend to have expertise in this area), but rather in the process of adaptation from stage-play into opera, and what this can tell us about the play's potential. In particular, I write in the context of a general argument that the play has long been underestimated by critics because they have concentrated almost exclusively on Falstaff instead of on the solid social localisation of the township of Windsor whose civically-minded citizens regard Falstaff, together with other 'outsider' figures, as dangerous interlopers and fortune-hunters. Since the people of Windsor regard Falstaff as an irritant rather than a hero it is against the grain for commentators to magnify his part and then criticise Shakespeare for not making him funny or large enough. At the same time, my argument incorporates the idea that Falstaff mirrors in comic fashion certain attributes which lie in the town's native-dwellers – acquisitive capitalism, a treatment of women as either property or marriage capital, and a general conflict between men and women. The wooing of Anne Page by three men, and Ford's violent jealousy, are the real centres of the play in my reading, and the Falstaff plot is a parodic counterpoint, a comic magnification of unconscious follies shared by others. His ritual punishment at Herne's oak outside Windsor at the end of the play is just as much a laying of unpleasant ghosts already in Windsor as an exorcism of Falstaff himself. Ford, for one, takes this point, and decides to mend his ways.

Nicolai, a Prussian born in 1810, died just two months after the first performance of his *Merry Wives* in 1849, when he was not yet thirty-nine years of age. The libretto is by Mosenthal, a young poet, but Nicolai's is the guiding hand throughout. High claims have been made for the music. The fairy scene is compared with Mendelssohn's *A Midsummer Night's Dream* (which Nicolai echoes), and other parts of the score are often said to be Mozartian in their musical ironies. One can also detect anticipations of Verdi (or, to put it another way, Verdi learned from Nicolai). The opera is not of simply antiquarian significance. Popular concert pieces include the Overture to Act One, the beautiful duet between Anne and Fenton, the fairy music in Windsor Forest and the rousing dance at the end.

Nicolai's version is, generally speaking, quite close to the play. It begins, however, at a point further into the plot than does Shakespeare, with the merry wives, Mistress Ford and Mistress Page discussing the outrageous letters of proposal they have received from Falstaff. This point of entry has been regarded as a flaw, at least by Winton Dean, who writes that '. . . it was a mistake to begin with the wives rather than Falstaff; neither the latter nor Ford appears before the linen-basket scene, which thus loses much of its impact' (p. 122). This is one voice among a chorus of criticisms finding Nicolai at fault for not making Falstaff more central and – as Dean frankly admits – not making the *men* central enough. The reading is insensitive to both Shakespeare and Nicolai. Nicolai no doubt was aware that Shakespeare had for a reason entitled his play *The Merry Wives of Windsor*, and the composer chooses to open with the merry wives. As so often in Shakespearian comedy, women are at the centre of the plotting and the emotional and moral design. Not only are the two wives central in their resistance to Falstaff and in the lesson they teach the jealous Ford, but also we find Mistress Quickly important to the plot (and cast at the end in the unlikely role of the Fairy Queen in the Forest), and of course Anne Page is the focus of the secondary plot concerning her marriage. Dean's criticism stems either from a priority he accords Verdi's *Falstaff* or from his frankly male-centred reading of the play. By placing 'Windsor' in his title, Shakespeare also carefully localises his play, implying that it will be a polyphonic representation of town life rather than a play about an individual, and this is exactly what we get in the play and in Nicolai's adaptation. By opening with the outrage and conspiracy of the women and delaying the entrance of Falstaff, Nicolai is exhibiting an order of faithfulness to the play which has not been given credit. There may well be a Mozartian influence here too, and comparisons can be made between Mozart and Shakespeare in their respective strong representations of women.

For musical contrast, Nicolai then gives us male voices, as the three suitors of Anne Page enter, and he shows Mr Page's refusal to countenance the claim of Fenton, who of course will be the successful candidate. Here Nicolai subtly alters Shakespeare's point. In the play, Page, as a solidly bourgeois character, has an innate suspicion of the aristocratic, courtly Fenton whom he regards as being after the dowry – which is in fact true initially as Fenton guilessly explains to Anne. Nicolai, perhaps as a Prussian not particularly *au fait* with the velleities of the English class system, and as a young man who was himself penniless most of his life, makes Page's objection hinge on the simple fact that Fenton has no money to bring to the marriage himself. (Nicolai does, incidentally, give the Prussian equivalent of the English courtly aristocrat by allowing Page to call Fenton a 'French turkey-cock'.) Nicolai simplified things by making Fenton (perhaps with some wish-fulfilment on his own part?) just poor but loving, and his refrain is 'Love will gain the victory'.

At last we meet Falstaff, whose musical presence is undoubtedly powerful when sung by a rich bass. Falstaff has been held back mainly to avoid the very possibility of his taking over the overall design which incorporates two equally important plots. Again, it is arguable that Nicolai, while changing details, is faithful to Shakespeare's comic vision in which rarely is a single character allowed to dominate the webs of amatory relationships and social interaction which he weaves.

We might also admire the economy of Nicolai's strategy, since, by giving us the women first, discussing Falstaff's letters, he is now given room to plunge straight into the strand of the plot which is based on Ford's jealous possessiveness over his wife. There is much foreshortening here, and the famous scene in which Falstaff is thrown into the river in the laundry-basket comes early enough to form a comic climax to Act One. Again, this may appear a flaw to critics who want to delay the scene to give it a more climactic effect than Shakespeare allows it to have, but on the other hand it maintains the symmetry Shakespeare gives us in his three punishments of Falstaff, culminating in the last in Windsor Forest at night, and in his repeated victories of the women over Ford. Nicolai also interestingly picks up a hint – perhaps unconsciously – from Shakespeare and transposes it into a different key. The men in the opera enter from a day's hunting. The image of Herne the Hunter certainly comes at the end of the play, and there are references at the beginning to Falstaff's killing of Shallow's deer, but Nicolai is here building into the picture Shakespeare's unobtrusive but real emphasis on the men's alignment with blood sports (bear-baiting, killing deer) and with duelling, adding up to the feeling that if the women are conspiratorial they need to be so because the men are potentially violent, a point to which we shall return.

The tightness of plotting relaxes in the first long scene in the Garter Inn between Falstaff and Ford disguised as Brook, opening with Falstaff's drinking song. Generally speaking the scene is neither musically interesting nor dramatically necessary in its length. When Nicolai returns to the wooing of Anne Page, he picks up the pace again, and allows the multiple points of view to echo and conflict in skilfully interwoven ensemble singing – a community of voices as the play is a community of interlocking and opposing relationships. The comedy of the parts of Slender and Caius heightens by contrast the lyrical beauty of the love-duet between Fenton and Anne, in a skilfully handled 'overhearing' scene reminiscent of Shakespeare's in *Love's Labour's Lost*. In the next scene, a duet is used to convey a very different spirit, as all the latent male violence erupts in Ford's jealous language while his wife laughs in his face.

The last scene of the play seems ready-made for conversion into opera, and it is almost certainly what drew the attention of so many composers. A play mostly written in prose moves into the register of poetry, all strands are brought together in an ensemble grouping where the community finally and ritualistically scourges itself of the tendencies embodied in Falstaff as people dressed up as fairies pinch him. Meanwhile, the love plot concerning Anne Page and Fenton is resolved in marriage. Nicolai's treatment does full justice to the scene, opening with mysterious mood-setting in the forest at night, using atmospheric harp, bells and high strings. The pinching of Falstaff is suitably rowdy and comic. Finally, the whole community joins for a triumphal and very well-known 'General Dance and Chorus', followed by the premonition of the wedding feast to follow – the celebratory, forgiving, Shakespearian ending.

Giuseppe Verdi had to all intents and purposes retired to the life of a farmer when, in 1889, in his mid-seventies, he received a libretto from Arrigo Boito, his collaborator on *Otello* two years previously. The libretto was based on *The Merry Wives of Windsor*. Verdi replied immediately, saying 'Excellent! Excellent! Before reading your sketch I wanted to re-read the "Merry Wives", the two parts of "Henry IV", and "Henry V", and I can only repeat: *Excellent*, for one could not do better than you have done.' And so was born *Falstaff*.

It is unfair to Nicolai to compare his measured, charming opera with Verdi's rumbustious *Falstaff* which is perhaps the greatest of all comic operas. I do not propose such a comparison, but instead I wish to distinguish between the two by saying that, while Nicolai's is an effective and faithful adaptation of Shakespeare's play into musical terms, Verdi's is a wholly new creation which, in its way, is a commentary upon *The Merry Wives* rather than an adaptation. In design and scope a more apt comparison would be Orson Welles' film *Chimes at Midnight*.

Both the title and the magnificent opening scene declare that Verdi's opera is not Shakespeare's story of Windsor under siege, but instead emphatically the story of Falstaff. Boito in his libretto dropped or conflated many of the characters and episodes from the play, and he made more prominent the characters of Falstaff and Mistress Quickly. The latter becomes a kind of organiser of the wives in their campaign against Falstaff, and a worthy female foil to him. One can readily acknowledge that these changes give a fundamental basis for a strong operatic structure, since opera can depend so much on paired, powerful voices. Drama and particularly comedy does not necessarily need only one or two central figures because of its emphasis on social relationships (see, for example, *A Midsummer Night's Dream*, *The Comedy of Errors* and *The Winter's Tale*). Instead, dramatic comedy can present a range of unfolding relationships building into an image of society, as I have argued is the case in *The Merry Wives of Windsor*. Equally, drama can tolerate considerably more complexity of unfolding plot and sub-plot than opera which depends on bold choices of major strands which must be given firm musical definition. Boito and Verdi made such choices appropriate to the medium in which they were working, by considerably simplifying the plot. For example, the wooing of Anne Page becomes far less significant and the episode of the Old Woman of Brainford is dropped altogether. In Verdi's opera, Falstaff and Mistress Quickly are foregrounded at the expense of other characters.

Another decision relates to the figure of Falstaff himself. Shakespeare in his play deliberately changes Falstaff's character by taking him away from his natural milieu in the Eastcheap tavern, the Boar's Head. In the play his seediness and threadbare wit are highlighted by contrast with the settled commercial and religious ethics of Windsor society, and there is little compensating elasticity of spirit. Just as he poses a threat to Windsor, so Windsor inadvertently robs him of his greatest strengths which, outside the yeasty warmth of London's pubs, are revealed as shallow egotism. To put it briefly, Windsor in the play basically lacks the sense of humour to appreciate a Falstaff. To be at his majestic best he needs an indulgent audience, and Shakespeare's sober, commercially-minded Windsor, not surprisingly, shows little but hostility to the disruptive presence in their midst. In the opera, however, Verdi, like Orson Welles and perhaps like himself in his own stance as political revolutionary, gives Falstaff back his subversively comic mastery. Verdi incorporates lines and passages from the *Henry IV* plays, where Falstaff stood so confidently (something which Nicolai did, admittedly, but far more sparingly than Verdi). His line at the end of the opera, ''Tis I, 'tis I alone, more is the pity, whose wit supply ye with the wherewithal to be witty', quoting from *2 Henry IV* 'I am not only witty in myself, but the cause that wit is in other men' (I. ii. 11), is a magisterial reprimand to lesser beings. At the same time, for us as Verdi's audience who *do* appreciate this vein in Falstaff, the line turns him into a comic scourge of dull sobriety rather than a scapegoat. It is he, in Verdi's opera, who is allowed the last, thematically central words, 'Jesting is a man's vocation, Wise is he who is jolly. . .'. In order to give substance to this claim, Boito incorporates some of the most famous of Falstaff's passages from the history plays in which he appears, such as the short soliloquy 'Sayst thou so, old Jack? go thy ways', the paean to the virtues of sherris sack, and the speech about honour (which Boito attaches to the dismissal of Pistol and Bardolph), into which Verdi builds multiple layers of rich musical comedy and tipsy magnificence. There are many other echoes, and even a borrowing from *As You Like It*, Jaques' 'All the world's a stage' speech. They build up a fascinating intertextuality which, incidentally, provides an interpretative commentary on Shakespeare's presentation of a character in different lights according to different contexts. The great critical debates about whether Falstaff is a sordid vice-figure or an inspired jester have been decisively arbitrated by Verdi and Boito in favour of the latter. This is not, however, a licence for us to ignore the genuine ambivalences in Shakespeare's respective presentations, nor to erase the distinctions between three quite separate plays, each with its own particular atmosphere, structure and guiding thematic concentrations. Critics usually say that Verdi has 'improved' *The Merry Wives* and that he has given us the 'real'

Falstaff. Neither assertion is true. He has not pretended to give us Shakespeare's *Merry Wives* but a new work based loosely on *The Merry Wives* and drawing on several others, and he has not given us Shakespeare's Falstaff but his own, an extrapolation from and amplification of the original.

Having made these points, which I regard as basic and important, we can in unencumbered fashion appreciate Verdi's own artistry. In musical terms the work can be considered as great as Shakespeare's is in literary and dramatic terms. The great genius Verdi demonstrates is to make the music itself into drama and drama into music, so that we learn far more about character and situation from the music than from the libretto. Characters are given musical signatures, such as the mocking melody of Mistress Quickly's archly mock-obsequious 'Reverenza' ('Your humble servant') and Falstaff's motif introduced in his address to Ford, 'Caro Signor Fontana'. Both recur in different contexts with different tonal significances. An expert on music speaks also of Falstaff's 'tendency to lean his weight on the key of C major in which the opera begins and ends' (Dean in Hartnoll, p. 126). The harmonic basis of the confident C major is commented on by most musical critics of the opera. The same commentator explains the opportunities for surprise which are possible within Verdi's technique of using cadence figures as motives. The crescendo of Ford's jealousy, 'O matrimonio: Inferno . . .' is reminiscent of chords in *Otello*, and also faithful tonally to Shakespeare, who in the character of Ford is anticipating his own Othello. The extraordinary capacity of opera, the one distinguishing it from drama, is its ability to portray many events simultaneously through different strands of music (in drama only one person at once can really talk and be heard). This is seen at its greatest in the climax of Act Two, when Falstaff is taken groaning out in the laundry-basket and emptied in the Thames, to the desperation of the impotently jealous, deluded Ford, the mocking of the triumphant wives, and at the same time the clandestine love-talk of Fenton and Nanetta, a virtuoso feat of composition from

Verdi. Towards the end we have the magical calm of the Fairy Queen's entrance – just before the storm of orchestration at the climax of the last Act, as the harsh vindictiveness of the fairies pinching Falstaff is enacted musically in pizzicato.

Vaughan Williams' *Sir John in Love* is very different again, demonstrating the apparently infinite potential of *The Merry Wives of Windsor* to inspire creative adaptation. Vaughan Williams composed it during a particularly rich period of musical output in 1924–8, although it had to wait until 1946 for its first full professional performance. In 1931, choral extracts from the opera were put together into the five-movement cantata *In Windsor Forest*. Vaughan Williams was spurred to write the opera partly in emulation of his favourite Falstaff opera, Nicolai's, and partly no doubt because he had grown fond of the Shakespearian play in 1913 when he was musical director to the Shakespeare Company at Stratford-upon-Avon under Frank Benson, during which period the company played *The Merry Wives* alongside *2 Henry IV*, *Henry V* and *Richard II*. In claiming licence to write yet another opera based on the play, Vaughan Williams playfully mentioned in his preface to the score that Shakespeare 'is fair game, like the Bible, and may be made use of nowadays even for advertisements of soap and razors'. He believed that Verdi, Nicolai and Holst (who wrote a one-act opera, *At the Boar's Head*, based on the history plays) had not exhausted the possibilities offered by the character of Falstaff and by the play.

Of all the versions, Vaughan Williams' is in some general ways the one closest to the play in narrative and tone. He retains all of Shakespeare's characters in their eccentricities, he maintains faithfully the plot-dimensions, and consequently diminishes the attention paid to Falstaff, who in fact turns out to be much mellower than either Verdi's or Shakespeare's character, and perhaps less egotistical and even genuinely 'in love'. These aspects have been criticised by opera critics, although as usual one feels that there is an implicit, prior judgement being made that Verdi is superior to Vaughan Williams instead of just being different. For the Shakespearian critic, it is no immediate condemnation that an adaptor trusts to the dramatist's plot-sense, instead of radically changing the shape.

In tone, it is clear that Vaughan Williams has made a conscious attempt to place the action unmistakably in England, right from its brief, autumnal overture. Vaughan Williams is also much kinder to Falstaff than even Shakespeare in making him both lovable and, however much a deceiver, a genuine lover of women in general. He is perhaps the composer who comes closest to capturing the 'deep-throated chuckle' found by A. C. Bradley in the fat knight of the *Henry IV* plays.

Of all three operas Vaughan Williams' is the one that tries to capture the atmosphere of Shakespeare's Windsor as an Elizabethan agricultural town close to community rituals. (Whether Elizabethan England was in reality ever so 'merry', organic and harmonised is a moot point, but it is an attractive legend.) In his strategy of building up such an atmosphere, Vaughan Williams commits the ultimate sin for many opera critics. He introduces into high opera humble English folk-songs and tunes. In each Act we get several folk-tunes (including 'Greensleeves', which is mentioned in the play), a psalm-tune and two English folk-dances, as well as many songs from other plays by Shakespeare and his contemporaries. With what sounds like disingenuous charm, Vaughan Williams justifies this provocative procedure in the following passage, where, incidentally, he speaks of Shakespeare's 'wonderful comedy':

> My chief object in *Sir John in Love* has been to fit this wonderful comedy with, I trust, not unpleasant music. In the matter of the use of folk-tunes, they only appear occasionally and their titles have no dramatic relevancy (except possibly in the case of 'John, come kiss me now'). When a particular folk-tune appeared to me to be the fitting accompaniment to the situation, I have used it.

When I could not find a suitable folk-tune, I have made shift to make up something of my own. I therefore offer no apology for the occasional use of a folk-song to enhance a dramatic point. If the result is successful I feel justified; if not, no amount of 'originality' will save the situation. However, the point is a small one, since out of a total of 120 minutes' music the folk-tunes occupy less than 15. . . .

An example of Vaughan Williams using with ironic richness a song from another play is when he allows Mistresses Ford and Page to be casually singing the 'cuckoo' song from the end of *Love's Labour's Lost* at the moment when Ford is beginning to suspect he has been cuckolded by Falstaff. He also maintains what is a thematic centre in Shakespeare's play, the battle between men and women, by, for example, including the rousing male song, 'When I was a bachelor, I lived a merry life, But now I am a married man and troubled with a wife', and by incorporating 'Sigh no more ladies, sigh no more, Men were deceivers ever . . .' from *Much Ado About Nothing*. What Vaughan Williams is mainly doing in all this is not only enhancing the comedy but ostentatiously anglicising and Elizabethanising his opera, consciously turning away from Verdi's powerful, comic farce into a lyrical idyll of middle-class life in an Elizabethan market town. He is taking back the play into English hands after its appropriation by the intense Prussian and the passionate Latin. This is perfectly consistent with the life's work of a composer who sought to adapt Shakespeare's songs into music with the English words and metres preserved, and with the tone as faithfully maintained as possible. It is worth noting that this opera stays more close to the actual lines of the play than either of the others.

It may still not be Shakespeare, for Vaughan Williams' version is perhaps too sentimental to capture the Shakespearian toughness of social analysis, but it is certainly no less authentically a creative adaptation than the other, very different masterpieces based on the wonderfully seminal play *The Merry Wives of Windsor*.

Epilogue

Audiences in the theatre have apparently never needed some ghost of a critic come from the grave to tell them how to enjoy *The Merry Wives of Windsor*, nor have the strictures of critics about the deficiencies of the play seemed to bother them. I have tried to remake the play as a reading experience more closely aligned with the ingenuous acceptance exercised by those theatre audiences. I hope also to have shown that there are ways in which the play can 'teach and delight' the reflective reader through effects that are over too quickly in the theatre to notice. In attempting to be open to the play's strengths I have probably understressed some awkwardnesses. To the reader, for example, the last section of the play, because it is so different in mode, can seem to be out of place. Magical transformation not only of events but of characters might require too jarring a gear-change. But then, if a director can splice the parts together, the play has done its job, and besides there are 'readings' available which can make such shifts lucid. T. W. Craik for one, in his Introduction to the latest edition of the play, makes a brave attempt which will convince some. Similarly, I have found in writing this book that there is at least one unintended truth in the opening epigraph from Engels that 'There is more life and reality in the first act of *The Merry Wives of*

Windsor alone than in all German literature', for (ignoring the disparagement of German literature) most of the arresting language and expression does indeed come 'in the first act'. The rest may be marvellous theatre and skilfully constructed scenic plotting, but admittedly it is closer to farce than to quotable drama: the special 'life and movement' of the middle acts come in their action rather than their speech-acts and consequently are perhaps less appreciated in reading than in performance. The force of Engels' 'alone' is to imply that he found delights throughout, but one could argue that their bases are different at each stage of the play.

To a reader generous enough to have read this book, I can advise only one thing. Go back to the play. Reread it, remake it, let its language play in the mind, its incidents delight. Let it alert us to the special strengths and limitations of women's roles in the 1590s and to the arrogance, jealousy and mercenariness of men. Write an opera based on it if you are able and inclined. 'Come, to the forge with it, then. Shape it. I would not have things cool' (IV. ii. 210–11).

Bibliography

Alexander, Peter (ed.), *William Shakespeare: The complete works* (Collins, London and Glasgow, 1951).

Anderson, Linda, *A Kind of Wild Justice: Revenge in Shakespeare's comedies* (University of Delaware Press, Newark, 1987), pp. 68–82.

Barton, Anne, 'Falstaff and the comic community', in Erickson, Peter and Kahn, Coppelia (eds.), *Shakespeare's 'Rough Magic': Renaissance essays in honor of C. L. Barber* (University of Delaware Press, Newark, 1985), pp. 131–48.

Berry, Ralph, *On Directing Shakespeare* (Hamish Hamilton, London, 1989).

Boas, Frederick S., *Shakespeare and his Predecessors* (Scribner, New York, 1896), pp. 292–343.

Bradbrook, Muriel C., *Shakespeare, The Craftsman* (The Clark Lectures 1968. Cambridge, 1979), pp. 75–96.

Brown, John Russell, *Shakespeare and his Comedies* (2nd edn, Methuen, London and New York, 1962), pp. 82–123.

Carroll, William C., *The Metamorphoses of Shakespearean Comedy* (Princeton University Press, New Jersey, 1985), pp. 178–204.

Chambers, E. K., *William Shakespeare: A study of facts and problems*, 2 vols. (Clarendon Press, Oxford, 1930).

Clark, Sandra, '"Wives may be merry and yet honest too": women and wit in *The Merry Wives of Windsor* and some other plays' in Mahon, John W. and Pendleton, Thomas A.

(eds.), *'Fanned and Winnowed Opinions': Shakespearean essays presented to Harold Jenkins* (Methuen, London and New York, 1987), pp. 249–67.

Craik, T. W. (ed.), *The Merry Wives of Windsor* (The Oxford Shakespeare, Oxford and New York, 1990).

Dean, Winton, 'Shakespeare and opera' in Hartnoll, Phyllis (ed.) *Shakespeare in Music: A collection of essays* (Macmillan, London, 1964), pp. 120–7.

Dekker, Thomas, *The Shoemaker's Holiday*, ed. R. L. Smallwood and Stanley Wells (Revels Plays, Manchester University Press and Johns Hopkins University Press, Manchester and Maryland, 1979).

Erickson, Peter, 'The Order of the Garter, the cult of Elizabeth, and class-gender tension in *The Merry Wives of Windsor*' in Howard, Jean E. and O'Connor, Marion F. (eds.), *Shakespeare Reproduced: The text in history and ideology* (Methuen, New York and London, 1987), pp. 116–42.

Evans, Bertrand, *Shakespeare's Comedies* (Clarendon Press, Oxford, 1960), pp. 68–117.

Fowler, James, 'David Scott's *Queen Elizabeth Viewing the Performance of the 'Merry Wives of Windsor' in the Globe Theatre* (1840)' in Foulkes, Richard (ed.), *Shakespeare and the Victorian Stage* (CUP, Cambridge, 1986), pp. 23–38.

French, Marilyn, *Shakespeare's Division of Experience* (Summit Books, New York, 1981), pp. 100–10.

Frye, Northrop, 'The argument of comedy' in *English Institute Essays, 1948*, pp. 58–93.

Green, William, *Shakespeare's 'Merry Wives of Windsor'* (Princeton University Press, New Jersey, 1962).

Green, William (ed.), *The Merry Wives of Windsor* (Signet Classic Shakespeare Series, New American Library, New York and Toronto, 1965).

Hartnoll, Phyllis (ed.) *Shakespeare in Music: A collection of essays* (Macmillan, London, 1964).

Hazlitt, William, '*The Merry Wives of Windsor*', in *The Characters of Shakespear's Plays* (1817) (Dent, London, 1906), pp. 250–2.

Hibbard, G. R. (ed.), *The Merry Wives of Windsor* (New Penguin Shakespeare, Penguin Books, Harmondsworth, 1973).

Hinely, Jan Lawson, 'Comic scapegoats and the Falstaff of *The Merry Wives of Windsor*', *Shakespeare Studies*, 15 (1982), pp. 37–54.

Honigmann, E. A. J., *Shakespeare: The lost years* (Manchester University Press, Manchester, 1985).

Hotson, Leslie, *Shakespeare versus Shallow* (Nonesuch Press, London, 1931).

Hunter, G. K., 'Bourgeois comedy: Shakespeare and Dekker' in Honigmann, E. A. J. (ed.), *Shakespeare and his Contemporaries* (Revels Plays Companion Library, Manchester University Press, 1986), pp. 1–15.

Jones, Emrys, *Scenic Form in Shakespeare* (Oxford, Clarendon Press, 1971).

Leggatt, Alexander, *Citizen Comedy in the Age of Shakespeare* (Toronto University Press, Toronto, 1973).

Nevo, Ruth, *Comic Transformations in Shakespeare* (Methuen, London and New York, 1980), pp. 142–61.

Nosworthy, J. M. *Shakespeare's Occasional Plays: Their origin and transmission* (Edward Arnold, London, 1965).

Oliver, H. J. (ed.), *The Merry Wives of Windsor* (New Arden Shakespeare, Methuen, London, 1971).

Rees, Joan, *Shakespeare and the Story* (Athlone Press, London, 1978).

Roberts, Jeanne Addison, 'The Merry Wives: suitably shallow but neither simple nor slender', *Shakespeare Studies*, 6 (1970), pp. 109–23.

Roberts, Jeanne Addison, '*The Merry Wives of Windsor* as a Hallowe'en play', *Shakespeare Survey*, 25 (1972), pp. 107–12.

Roberts, Jeanne Addison, 'Falstaff in Windsor Forest: villain or victim?', *Shakespeare Quarterly*, 26 (1975), pp. 8–15.

Roberts, Jeanne Addison, *Shakespeare's English Comedy: 'The Merry Wives of Windsor'* (University of Nebraska Press, Lincoln, Nebraska, 1979).

Salingar, Leo, *Shakespeare and the Traditions of Comedy* (CUP, Cambridge, 1974).

Vickers, Brian, *The Artistry of Shakespeare's Prose* (Methuen, London), pp. 89–170.

Wells, Stanley and Taylor, Gary (eds.), *William Shakespeare: The complete works (The Oxford Shakespeare)* (Clarendon Press, Oxford, 1986).

Wilson, John Dover, *Shakespeare's Happy Comedies* (2nd edn, London, 1969), pp. 76–93.

Woodbridge, Linda, *Women and the English Renaissance: Literature and the nature of womankind, 1540–1620* (Harvester Wheatsheaf, Hemel Hempstead, 1984).

Index